Praise for Old Times Not Forgotten

What a memory jog into the fun-filled days of my own innocent Southern childhood. Each story is simply uplifting and good for one's soul . . . A "Song of the South." —Donna Kirkland Cantrell

People from Mississippi like to tell stories. Sam and I grew up in the same hometown. That being said, I can attest to the fact that the stories in this book are absolutely the truth. They are delightful, and so is Sam!
—Sarah Wilkinson

Sam's stories…have brought laughter and a few tears. His Mississippi heritage is a rich source of vibrant stories. —Lucy Majors, co-author of *Baby Boy Majors*

A wonderful collection of small-town Mississippi tales that will entertain anyone curious about the deep South and its culture. Sam finds humor and irony in so many everyday experiences he has loved and embedded in his memory. He's a genuine "Mississippi boy" willing to share an appreciation of his eventful life and journey through it. —Beverly McKenzie

Sam is a born storyteller. From his early years growing up in Mississippi, his high school adventures in Oak Ridge, Tennessee, and his experiences as a football hero at Ole Miss, Sam has collected a lifetime of engaging stories. They are laced with Sam's natural humor and embedded with his profound wisdom and ethical values, which propelled his success as a healthcare executive. This book is entertainment at its best! You are guaranteed to enjoy getting to know Sam as much as I have! —Lisa Atkinson

Old Times Not Forgotten

Old Times Not Forgotten

As Told by a Son of the South

Samuel Walton Owen

Knoxville, Tennessee, USA
crippledbeaglepublishing.com

Cover art by Roger Ryskamp
Cover design by Maria Loysa-Bel Nueve- de los Angeles

Paperback ISBN 978-1-958533-58-1, 978-1-958533-60-4
Hardcover ISBN 978-1-958533-59-8, 978-1-958533-61-1
ePub ISBN 978-1-958533-62-8

Library of Congress Control Number: 2023922868

Printed in the United States of America

Disclaimer: I'm often correct but sometimes off a smidge. I took creative license to fill in gaps. This book is not a documentary. It's a collection of memories as I best recall them. They make me happy, sad, sentimental, and glad. Some I want to relive. Some I don't. The events, people, and dialogue are what they are—*Old Times Not Forgotten.*

Stories

Great Memories

Great memories are without a doubt one of our most cherished assets in life. They are always there to enjoy. All you have to do is call them up, go to that marvelous filing cabinet in the recesses of your mind, and retrieve them when you want them. Your memories will be there to make a gray day bright or to take you on the bounding main. They can take you to a romantic tryst. Memories can recall a soothing rain, and they can do almost anything to make your life complete. They are free. All you have to do is call upon them and tell them where to meet you.

Over the years, my fabulous wife Judy has encouraged me to write a book about my eventful life. I really didn't want to do that. I don't consider myself to be an author. That said, I have written a beaucoup of love letters, love notes, poems, and stories to Judy telling her how much I love her and how much she means to me. I do this almost every day of my life with her.

One day, Corinne Owen, my second oldest granddaughter, called me and said, "BoBo, I need to talk to you about something very important."

Of course, I obliged her. I quickly learned the reason for her call. She wanted to encourage me to write about my incredible life's journey. How could I ignore those requests from my granddaughter and my wonderful wife? I couldn't. Consequently, I am now trying to become a storyteller using the written word rather than oral conveyance. Actually, I believe that I have evolved to become pretty good at this game. I now realize that I enjoy writing about my life because it brings back so many fond memories and emotions. I'm not going to try to be a one and done writer, but at my age I realize that my runway isn't quite as long as it used to be. I hope you enjoy reading my stories as much as I have enjoyed writing them. This once-dreaded project has now become an endeavor of love. For that, I thank Judy for her encouragement and her enduring love. I also want to thank Corinne for her subtle yet forceful impetus.

I also want to thank two people for their unselfish help and friendship. First, let me say: Billy Humphrey, you are a remarkable man. With a *red ink* tweak here and a *red ink tweak* there, you improve my work without fanfare. With subtle competence you make my words flow so smoothly. I truly appreciate your help and your friendship.

Sandra Whitten Plant, my Oak Ridge High School friend and classmate, thank you for inviting me to join your writing group. If you hadn't done that, I wouldn't be doing this. I also thank you for introducing me to Billy. I love our time together when we edit each other's stuff. You are a valued encourager and friend. You are also adept at using your *red ink pen* to edit my work. Did you teach Billy, or did he teach you? Either way, it works for me, and I thank you for the *red ink edits*.

Your friend,

Sam

Hoboing to Somewhere

One sure thing about living in a small Mississippi town like Louisville in 1951 is there's not a lot to do. Summer days were occupied by fishing, riding bikes, and just plain messing around. One of my favorite 'messing arounds' was to line up pennies on top of the railroad tracks of the Gulf, Mobile & Ohio Railroad. Johnny, Lance, Doll Baby, Flournoy and I would gather up as many pennies as we could find, line 'em up on top of the track, and wait for the train's huge engines to smash 'em flat.

Whenever we heard the engineers blow the first whistle announcing the arrival of the GM&O's freight train, we took off lickety-split to our favorite spot near the tracks. That's where we lined up our pennies (whenever we had some). After the train rolled over them, the coins were flattened out, making Abraham Lincoln look like a doofus, all funny looking and distorted.

On this particular day things were a little different because everything was just moving slowly. The GM&O was moving slowly. Johnny and I were late and moving slowly. We headed to the spot near the tracks to line up our three pennies.

After placing our pennies on the track we noticed the doors of several of the boxcars were open. That's when I had a great idea. I yelled to Johnny, "Come on, let's get in one of those boxcars and ride down to The Railroad Hotel and get off." That's where the replacement crews stayed. The train always stopped there for the change of crews and to get some water in the tanks of the engines before steaming toward Philadelphia, Mississippi, some thirty-five miles down the line on its way to somewhere.

We decided that was a great idea since the train was moving slowly enough for us to pick out a boxcar and climb in. Johnny looked at me with wild, blazing eyes and said, "Sam, I'm glad you came up with this idea. I ain't never been on a train before. How fast will it go?"

I told him, "Heck, I don't know, but it sho does beat walking to Philadelphia." All I thought was, *We are now officially hobos!* There was one fly in the ointment. Our mamas and daddies had forbidden us to do what we were doing. We rationalized that we were only going to do this once. Besides, with the GM&O rolling so slowly, jumping off when the train stopped for the crew change and water fill up would be easy as pie.

As we sat there dangling our legs out of the gaping door and enjoying our ride to The Railroad Hotel, something strange happened. The train's cars lurched forward. The speed of the train picked up rapidly. The steep incline of the ground beside the tracks wouldn't allow us to jump off the train. I had never seen the train go that fast. "What's going on?" Johnny asked.

I knew the answer to that question in a flash when Johnny and I watched The Railroad Hotel fly past us in a blur. For some unknown reason, the crews didn't change, the GM&O engines didn't get their thirst quenched, and the newest hobos on the rails were about to learn a severe lesson. We were hoboing somewhere. Where in the world were we going? The GM&O engineers knew, but we didn't. That's when we realized that we may never return from this nightmare. We had no idea that the train's destination was New Orleans, Louisiana.

Unbeknownst to Johnny and me, someone had seen us jump into one of the train's boxcars. Thank goodness that person called my mama to tell her about our exploits. Immediately, Mama called The Railroad Hotel to ask them to tell me to stay put until she got there. The hotel's manager on the other end of the line said, "Miss Corinne, it's too late. The train didn't stop here on this trip. It's on its way to New Orleans, and I don't have a way to contact the engineer. Do you know anyone in Philadelphia who could call the station master there to stop the train?"

Thankfully, Mama's sister, Hallye Parkes McCauley, lived in Philadelphia. When she heard the story about her favorite nephew, she started laughing hysterically. After gathering herself, she said, "We'll get the train stopped, but what do you want us to do with Hobo Sam and his hobo friend?"

Mama's answer was curt and quick, "If y'all get that train stopped, you tell our hobos that their hoboing days are over, but their nightmare is just about to begin. I'm on my way to get them."

Hallye called her husband, Josh, who was the founder and president of the First National Bank of Philadelphia. Uncle Josh was a wonderful man. He was nice, fun, and a fabulous uncle. He would do anything for you if asked. He was now being asked.

Aunt Hallye told Uncle Josh the hobo story. It took several minutes for him to stop laughing and get his breath back. Once he did, he told Aunt Hallye, "I had a great idea hit me while you were telling me about Sam and his hobo buddy. I'm amazed I could think 'cause I was laughing so hard." Uncle Josh's idea was about to become a reality. He called the sheriff's office.

As the huge GM&O engines started rolling through Philadelphia, Sheriff Mars was standing by the railroad tracks where the train stopped on occasion but not routinely. He was waving at the engineers to stop the train. Thank the Lord he was successful.

The brakes squealed and the cars bucked, groaned, and rocked back and forth. The train came to a noisy, sooty stop.

That's when Johnny and I saw the sheriff with his huge, leashed German Shepherd at his side. The sheriff marched straight toward us and our boxcar. He unholstered his huge pistol as he walked.

He yelled at us, "Put your hands in the air and don't move a muscle. Stay in that car. You're under arrest."

I almost vomited. Johnny started whimpering, "I'm gonna throw up!" We didn't know what to do. I tried to say something nice to the sheriff, but no words came out of my mouth. Johnny tried to ask me a question, but he had the same problem.

The big German Shepherd didn't have that problem. It was snarling and barking furiously. The sheriff could barely hold him back with his leash.

If we get out of this mess, I will…

The sheriff interrupted my thoughts. He yelled, "Lay face down with your heads toward me so we can handcuff you."

About that time a deputy sheriff climbed into the boxcar and put the cuffs tight around our wrists as we held our hands behind our backs. We were now hardened criminals.

I wanted my mama, but I didn't really want my mama. She would want to kill us, but I didn't think she would. On second thought….

The sheriff and his deputy got Johnny and me out of the box car, and we headed to his police car. I asked the sheriff, "Where we going?"

His response scared the hell out of me. "You two are going to jail to await your trial."

Johnny and I threw up on that spot. How was I going to get in touch with Mama? I sure as heck wasn't gonna call Daddy.

The police car pulled up in front of the police station. Then we were booked. After that, the sheriff informed us, "You get one call. Who do you want to call?"

We both started crying as the door to the station opened. In walked Aunt Hallye, Uncle Josh, and Mama. Uncle Josh asked Sheriff Mars, "How long will they have to stay in jail?"

The sheriff said, "I don't know for sure; Judge Cook is out of town on vacation for two weeks."

That did it! I was doomed. Johnny was too. We decided this was our last time to hobo or to put pennies on railroad tracks.

Uncle Josh, Aunt Hallye, and Sheriff Mars orchestrated this entire episode. It was elaborate, but worth it. Johnny and I learned our lesson. We were released to the custody of our parents. Our record was expunged. Charges were dismissed.

I was eighty-two years old on August 4, 2023, and I haven't put pennies on a railroad track or hoboed since that day in 1951. That's seventy-three years of crime-free living.

The Bully: Taking Care of Bidness

The Playground Store had the best cheeseburgers in the state of Mississippi. Maybe the world. It was located directly across the street from the school's huge playground where I had so much fun every day during recess.

This day had a different feel to it. A new boy had recently moved to town from nearby Macon, Mississippi. He was bigger than the rest of us boys in the fifth grade, and he was flaunting it. On his first visit to the playground he went up to each of us boys, pushing us, slapping our cheeseburgers out of our hands, and slyly punching us in our stomachs so the teachers could not see.

Yep! Louisville now had its first known bully, and nobody liked it. None of us were brave enough to take him on. That's exactly how he wanted things to be; that just emboldened him to bully us more with his cowardly stunts.

The bully found that he could get away with whatever he wanted to do because he was an expert at snowing and swooning the teachers. They appeared to be oblivious to his bullying crap because of his bootlicking antics, and all the teachers thought he was cute.

As the days went by, things got worse. He had now decided to expand his bullying territory from the school's playground to the main sidewalk that most of us used to go to and from school, even when we were on our bikes. Also, he would hide in the big hedges along the way and jump out to beat up us smaller boys. He would make us wreck our bikes. He even took the chain off of the sprockets. He would mess up our clothes. His favorite prank was to rip the collars of our shirts if we wore collared shirts. He did that to me, and I didn't do anything about it because I was afraid of him. Pure and simple, I was just like everyone else.

When I walked into the kitchen on a glorious fall afternoon with my shirt collar ripped and hanging down and my right eye red from the blow from Bully Boy, I was unexpectedly greeted by my daddy. He was sitting at the kitchen table, drinking a cup of coffee, and waiting for me. At first, he didn't utter a word to me for what seemed like an eternity. He just stared at me with a disgusted expression. He could tell that I had been crying. Finally, he asked, "What in the hell happened to you?"

I thought about lying to Daddy by telling him I had been playing football and that my shirt collar got torn. Then I decided that lying to my daddy would bring more wrath than any bully could dish out.

I came clean. I told Daddy every gory detail between sobs. He listened patiently and intently until I was finished. After a pause, he said calmly, "Okay Doc, go get cleaned up and come out on the porch. We need to have a daddy/son talk." Daddy always called me Doc. It was his nickname of endearment for me.

After my shower I joined Daddy on the front porch swing. We had a long, sincere conversation about life in general and how to deal with certain difficulties along life's highways. When our conversation was over, he stood up and hugged me close to him. He kissed me on top of my head and said, "Doc, you know how much I love you. You'll thank me for this later in your life when I'm long gone."

That hit me in my gut like a ton of bricks. I really did feel much better now, but I didn't like the "when I'm gone" comment. Daddy always told me how much he loved me, how proud he was of me, and how much he enjoyed talking with me. But he could leave out the "after I'm gone" comment, and I told him that. He then added a stunner as he left the front porch swing, "I'll pick you up at school tomorrow at 3:30. You're going to fix your bully problem once and for all." He went inside the house and left me to mull over that last comment.

What did he mean? How can I fix the bully problem? He didn't insinuate that he was going to go talk to the bully's folks. He just left me dangling out there in space without any particular instructions. That was that. That was also his intention. I began to wonder and ponder. My stomach had butterflies the size of bald eagles and knots as big as my fists competing for space in the center of my gut. I hated that feeling, but ironically, I did feel a lot better. I didn't sleep much that night. I tossed and turned, wondering and pondering.

The next morning, I didn't eat one bite of my favorite breakfast. I didn't touch any of the fried eggs, country ham, cheese grits, red-eye gravy, or Mama's fluffy biscuits. I was too anxious about how I was gonna fix my bully problem. We didn't talk about anything during breakfast. Nobody said a word after our "Good mornings." Total silence.

Finally, Daddy broke the silence as he was leaving for work when he said, "Come on Doc, you're riding with me. I'll give you a ride to school since I'm picking you up after school today. You won't be needing your bike." My immediate reaction was, *Oh crap, he hasn't forgotten.*

It was a long day at school. I didn't learn a thing. My mind was wandering, pondering, and rehearsing my next encounter with the bully, whom I successfully avoided the entire day.

The school bell rang at 3:30 p.m. to dismiss us. I reluctantly got up from my desk. With sweaty palms, I started walking slowly toward the main entrance of the red brick schoolhouse. I was hoping Daddy had forgotten and wasn't there. When I exited the school into the sunlight of the beautiful fall day, I saw him waiting for me in his black Ford pickup truck in front of the school. My hopes were dashed. My heart started racing a mile a minute. "Oh crap, why is he here?" I asked myself. I had forgotten that I didn't ride my bike to school.

As I nervously approached the truck, Daddy said, "Get in Doc, we're going for a little ride to talk about some things." As he drove off, he began talking and I began listening intently, oblivious to our location. Finally, the black Ford pickup stopped. Lo and behold, we were sitting in front of the bully's house. Daddy turned off his truck's engine. He sat there silent for a moment and then turned to me. Looking me square in the eyes, he said, "Now, you go take care of bidness. I'll wait for you right here. Remember what I told you about fixing this bully problem. You fix it with him, or I'll fix it with you. It's your choice."

I gulped; I was absolutely scared to death. I reluctantly said, "Yessir," and slowly opened the door and got out of the pickup. I actually thought about running off, but my knees were too weak. My legs felt like rubber bands. I started walking meekly toward the front door of the bully's house. My gut was churning and tied in knots. My palms were wringing wet. My heart was pounding so hard it sounded like a bass drum in the high school band at a football game. I had never done anything like this in my life. *Can I do it?* I wondered to myself. I certainly didn't know then what I know now.

I knocked on the door.

The playground hotshot appeared at the screen door. It was the bully! He looked bigger and more intimidating than ever. His cocky smirk and voice delivered an even more arrogant message, "What do you want Pun…?"

The "K" never made it out of his mouth. My right fist had just rearranged his cocky nose in the center of his face. His nose resembled a hot baked potato after being smushed to receive lots of creamy butter. His nose was now a flat, bloody blob in the middle of his cocky face. Blood spewed everywhere. It was on the walls. It was all over his white tee shirt. It was on my white tee shirt. Shrieking in pain, he dropped to his knees. Soon he was groaning and crying and lying on his side on the floor. Then he was flat on his back and crying and screaming, "Why'd you do that? You broke my nose!"

I straddled him and stood over him for what seemed to be forever rather than a few seconds. Finally, I leaned down near his bloody face and said, "Don't you ever bully me again, you asshole!"

I stood up and turned to head back to Daddy's pickup truck. I heard the engine crank over the sobs and groans coming from behind the screen door. As I started down the steps on my way to the truck, I realized that my palms weren't sweaty. My heart wasn't pounding. The knots in my stomach were untied. The eagle-sized butterflies were long gone. A smile crept across my face. I was content. I had just taken care of bidness once and for all! The Bully had just become an irrelevant piece of crap.

News spread fast. Everyone came up and congratulated me the next day at school. The Bully never bullied me again—or anyone else for that matter. In fact, he became an obscure, ignored, and pitiful nobody. The irony of the story is that I don't even remember his name.

Now you know what my daddy had told me during our short ride to the bully's house. He just told me how to take care of *bidness*. I did precisely what he told me to do.

That incident was the only time in my life that I ever experienced bullying. The word must have gotten out and traveled far and wide. "Don't Bully Sam! He'll kick your ass."

Maybe our current generations could learn something about dealing with bullies from this story. Instead of moaning, whimpering, and cowering to Mama and Daddy, just take care of your own damn *bidness*! It worked for me.

Sam Meets God

In 1950 my folks decided that I should become a Cub Scout. I was nine years old at the time. My mama and daddy felt that I needed to broaden my activities beyond fishing, riding bikes, and playing baseball. I really didn't want to be a Cub Scout because I didn't want to have to work on the stupid projects to win awards and merit badges. I had absolutely no interest in hook weaving potholders, plaiting lanyards for keys, and stuff like that. After a little bit of coddling by my folks, the tone of the discussion shifted dramatically from, "We would like for you to consider becoming a Cub Scout," to, "Your first Cub Scout Den meeting is tomorrow at three o'clock."

Suddenly, I realized that my smart-ass, obstinate attitude just might win me a trip to the huge hedge that enclosed our backyard. The purpose of that trip would be to cut Mama the perfectly sized switch for her attitude adjustment session with me. Right then and there I surrendered. Mama had spoken. She knew how to make sure that I selected the best switch. She also knew how to use it to get my attention and make me dance all around her to avoid the switching. That never worked, so I decided to make one last, pitiful plea to my mother. I told her that the only way that I would join the Cub Scouts was if Mrs. Libby would be my den mother. That bit of flippancy didn't sit well with Mama. Her retort was classic Eva Corinne Parkes Owen. She said to me, "Honey, that is really quite noble of you. Now you run on out yonder to the hedge and bring me a nice big switch. You know the kind I want, so run out yonder and hurry back." The Cub Scout debate was over. I picked the right switch. I did my dance. I was going to be a Cub Scout.

Mrs. Libby was a wonderful, sweet lady. She was David's mother. David was one of my best friends. Mrs. Libby was also a great cook. She would make stuff that I had never even heard before, but it was always good. A lot of her food was made from recipes she had collected from Brooklyn, New York. Mrs. Libby was married to Mr. Frank Libby.

Mr. Frank was a very nice man, and all of David's buddies really did like him. Mr. Libby also owned the only shoe store in town, Libby's Shoes. Everyone in Louisville, Winston County, and surrounding counties bought their shoes from Mr. Frank. He was entertaining, and he made going to the shoe store fun. Most of the time, getting some new shoes was pure drudgery, but not with Mr. Frank.

Mama always wanted to see several different pairs of shoes on me so she could pick out the best ones. She would have me try on loafers, lace ups, black ones, brown ones, and so on. If it had been up to me, I would have been out of there in five minutes wearing a new pair of Converse tennis shoes. I hated buying new dress-up shoes and new clothes because it took so much time away from riding my bike, fishing, and playing with my friends.

One thing was certain. Mr. Libby would always do funny little things to make you laugh while he was trying on your shoes. He loved to put paper in the toes of the shoes to make you think your foot had grown a lot since the last time you bought shoes.

Then he would get some more shoes that were way too big. Then he would scratch his head and tell you that he didn't have any shoes that fit, so he would have to get Mr. Floyd to make a pair of shoes down at his harness and livery stable. (Mules and wagons were still popular modes of transportation during the 1940s and 1950s.) When he saw the perplexed look on my face, he would laugh and tell me the reason that my shoes didn't fit was because Buster Brown and his dog Tige lived in there together. He would then laugh until tears ran down his face. That's when we had to recite with him the Slogan for Buster Brown Shoes, "Hi, I'm Buster Brown. I live in a shoe. This is my dog Tige. He lives in there, too." Then came another burst of laughter and my new pair of shoes. That was Mr. Frank's shoe trick! Mr. Frank came to work early and stayed late. He was a little bit like Buster Brown; he practically lived in his shoe store. Mrs. Libby was always by his side, so I suppose she lived there too.

Other than being the only shoe merchant in Louisville, Mississippi, Mr. Frank had two other distinctions. One was that he was the only Jew from Brooklyn, New York, living within hundreds of miles of Louisville, Mississippi. Two, Mrs. Libby wasn't Jewish. She was from Mississippi, and Mr. Libby called her his pretty Mississippi "Shiksa." Let me assure you that those distinctions were both firsts in this part of the world, and they will probably never be replicated.

I really didn't know anything about people from Brooklyn, New York. I certainly didn't know any Jewish people other than Jesus and his buddies. Of course, I never met them except through church, Sunday school, and the Bible. The only people I had ever heard of who were from Brooklyn were Duke Snyder, Peewee Reese, Jackie Robinson, Carl Furillo, Gil Hodges, Junior Gilliam, Roy Campanella, Carl Erskine, and Don Newcombe. I knew they lived there because they played baseball for the Brooklyn Dodgers. The only Jew I knew personally was Mr. Frank. He didn't play baseball. He sold shoes in Mississippi.

Now, the first question always asked of Mr. Frank when people learned he was from Brooklyn was, "How in the world did you get to Louisville, Mississippi, from Brooklyn?"

His response was always the same. "I married my Shiksa from Mississippi." Nobody knew what Shiksa meant, so instead of appearing to be stupid, they would just mutter under their breath and respond with something like, "Oh, I see." Then they would drop the subject. That discussion was over, but my mama and Mrs. Libby were dear friends. My mama knew more, but she didn't gossip about what she knew.

The real reason that Mr. Frank left Brooklyn was that he was from an extremely strict, religious, orthodox Jewish family. His father was a Rabbi who wore some really unusual looking clothes. He wore shawls, a big black hat with a flat brim, a full beard, and little pig tails hanging down like sideburns. I had never seen him or met him. Heck, I really didn't know what a Rabbi was. I am just repeating what my good friend David Frank told me about his grandfather.

David told me that his daddy had met his mom in New York City, and they fell in love. He told me that when Mr. Frank decided that he was going to ask Mrs. Libby to marry him, that threw his family into a tornado of religious upheaval. Rabbi Libby told his son that if he pursued the marriage of this Shiksa he would be banished from the family, never to be seen or heard from again.

He did and he was.

That's really sad, but that was Louisville's gain and Brooklyn's loss. That's the reason Louisville had one of, if not the best, shoe stores in the state of Mississippi and the only Jewish shoe peddler for hundreds of miles around these parts.

Mrs. Libby decided to assemble a good group of boys to join her son, David, in the newly created Cub Scout Pack #124, Den #3. She was the Den mother. Mrs. Libby was extremely creative and always had interesting projects for the scouts to work on at the meetings. Some of her projects would be concluded by the end of the Den meeting, and we could take them home to show our parents what we had accomplished that day.

Some projects were more elaborate than others and could take several meetings to complete. We took such projects home to our mamas so they could ooh and aah over a potholder, plaited lanyard for keys, or some other exquisite trinket that would wind up in a box to be opened years later while cleaning out the attic.

Regardless, the outcome always drew praises at home. That may have been because our moms really liked what we had done, or they were just grateful for the relief that someone else had to put up with our mischief for several hours once a week. I do know that my mama never let me miss a den meeting. Everyone appeared to be very happy when the meeting day arrived.

This particular day Den #3 Scouts had something in store for them that would make one particular project unforgettable. A year earlier, Mrs. Libby had selected a truly unique project for us to undertake. This project was more difficult than any we had ever tackled before. We had been transformed into planters. No, we weren't going to become cotton farmers or soybean planters. We became specialized planters and planted something very special to me. I had persuaded Mrs. Libby to plant one of my favorite plants because I loved its fruit. It was difficult to find this particular fruit because grocery stores didn't have it available very often, if ever. Mrs. Libby let us plant pomegranate bushes in her yard beside her house. She was reluctant at first, but she finally agreed to the request, and now she was glad she did.

When we arrived at the Den meeting this bright, sunny, summer day, Mrs. Libby was obviously excited. She said she had two pieces of news to share with us. It appeared that she was more thrilled about the first news item than she was for the other. In her usual calm manner, she had us close our eyes and carefully walk to a particular spot in her yard and take a seat in the grass. When she told us to open our eyes, we were looking at three beautiful pomegranate bushes that were loaded with beautiful, orangish-red, plump pomegranates. We all clapped and cheered. After the noise settled down, she asked us all to stand and promise on our Cub Scout honor that we would not bother her pomegranates. Of course, we all did as she asked. I led the resounding oath of obedience as we all recited that, on our Honor, we would not bother her beautiful pomegranates.

The next item of news was that David's grandfather from Brooklyn, New York, had surprised the Libbys with an unannounced visit. Mr. Frank's Rabbi daddy had come to Louisville to reconcile matters with his son. Mrs. Libby asked all of us to hold the noise down so we wouldn't disturb David's granddaddy because he was taking a nap after his long, hard trip from Brooklyn. Of course, we said we would do as she asked, even though none of us knew him or knew what he looked like.

Then Mrs. Libby took us back around to the other side of the house to the work area for us to commence our project for the day. Frankly, my mind wasn't on the project. I didn't even hear what we were supposed to do. I was thinking about my favorite fruit. I was thinking about those beautiful, orangish-red, plump pomegranates packed full of those fat little red seeds filled with tart juice that exited the plant's interior in juicy clumps that could explode in the mouth. My mouth was puckering as I thought about the tart, juicy explosion. Right then and there I made my furtive move. I was going pomegranate hunting.

Unnoticed, I made my way toward the other side of the house where the pomegranates were gracefully guarding the side yard. The weight of the juicy fruits almost broke the branches of each tree. I could help relieve that burden, and that was my reason for disobeying Mrs. Libby's request.

As I stealthily approached the pomegranates to make my move, my eyes were focused on one particular fat, beautiful, orangish-red, plump pomegranate up rather high in the tree. I was going to have to really stretch on my tiptoes to get that baby. I was just below the windows of the guest bedroom in the Libby house. That would be the room where Mr. Libby's father was taking his nap. As I clasped my fingers around the fruit, I caught a glimpse of movement in the window above the pomegranate bushes. Somewhat startled, I slowly raised my eyes and looked up at the window of the guest bedroom. My fingers had just seized the pomegranate in my hand as I was about to pluck the juicy morsel from the tree.

That's when my eyes focused on a large figure standing in the window above me and watching my every move. The person who occupied that large body was dressed in what appeared to be black robes draping over a large, barrel-chested body. A wide, flat-brimmed, black hat was perched on top of his huge head and was at least two sizes too small. A full gray and silver beard covered the face of the imposing figure. There was no movement by either of us. I was still grasping my beautiful, orangish-red, plump pomegranate. The stranger in the window was still glaring at me. The little curly pigtail sideburns were scary looking and accentuated the face of this odd-looking creature.

I decided to make my move. I snatched the beautiful, orangish-red, plump pomegranate from the bush. Just as I did, the mystery figure raised both arms up and began shaking all ten of his fingers at me. That is when I threw the beautiful, orangish-red, plump pomegranate to the ground. I screamed to the top of my lungs. I ran to get on my trusty Schwinn Black Phantom

Bicycle with silver fenders and red and black paint trim, and pedaled home as fast as my nine-year-old legs would go.

Finally, I was home.

Now safe on the other side of town, I burst into my house and yelled for my mama. She wasn't there. I was crying and scared to death. I didn't know what to do. I picked up the telephone which had a straight shafted body and was rather tall. It did not have dialing capability. The earpiece dangled from the side of the body of the phone box. I learned into the phone, put the earpiece to my ear, and spoke into the microphone asking the central operator, Miss Carter, where my mama was. Miss Carter told me Mama was playing bridge at Ivell's house. I was totally scared to death. I ran to my room and got under the covers on my bed and waited for Mama to come home.

Finally, after waiting and hiding for what felt like years, I heard my mama's voice when she asked, "Sam, Honey, are you home?"

Yelling and crying, I told her that I was in my room. Soon she opened my door and immediately realized something was terribly wrong. She rushed to my bedside and sat down on the side of the bed. She took my hand in hers and asked me what was wrong. She was visibly alarmed.

I was too. I told her in great detail about my experience. My explanation came through sobs and gasps for air. After hearing the gory details, I told Mama that I was going to hell because I had lied to Mrs. Libby. I told her that I had given Mrs. Libby my Scout's Honor that I wouldn't touch her beautiful, orangish-red, plump pomegranates, and I went back on my word. Then I told her that I picked one pomegranate, and I was going for the second one when I saw God watching me, and God's going to send me straight to Hell, probably before I die.

My mother let go of my hand, stood up, and left the room in haste without uttering a single word. She was in a big hurry to get out of my room. That's when I knew I was doomed. God was going to send me to hell, and my mama had abandoned me. Things were spinning out of control as if I were in a whirlpool in a vast ocean.

I wasn't aware that the reason Mama left the room in such a hurry was that she was about to choke to death to try to keep from bursting out laughing at my epic story. A short time later, after she had called Mrs. Libby to tell her the story, she returned to my room, where I was still hiding in my bed under the covers. Mama explained to me that God was Mr. Frank Libby's father.

From that day forward, I knew precisely what a Rabbi was because I had seen one. My mama took me over to the Libbys' house for me to meet God. He was a really nice man, but he was unusual in several ways. First, he dressed funny. He talked funny. And he really wasn't funny. He appeared to be quite stern, but he loved the story my mama related to him about his role as God. Mr. Frank Libby and his father reconciled their relationship to some acceptable degree. Rabbi Libby returned to Brooklyn, New York. We never saw him again.

History's Made

Small Mississippi towns were remarkable places during the years of my youth. When I was growing up, they all had similar characteristics. Main street parking was random and not always between the lines. Pickup trucks, not sedans, were the predominant mode of transportation, not to mention mule-drawn wagons. Yep, that's the way it was, and I loved it. Too bad things have changed to the point that a mule-drawn wagon is now a photo op rather than an everyday mode of transportation.

I can't speak with any authority on the way social customs and mores operate in today's small-town society, but I can talk about the time when I was there. It was special and unique. One thing that existed in each of those little hamlets was a small group of young boys and an occasional girl who were inseparable, a la, The Little Rascals of movie fame.

The Little Rascals were made up of Spanky, Stymie, Alfalfa, Cookie (the girl), and Buckwheat, who was colored. Our gang in Louisville was made up of Johnny, Lance, Doll Baby (our only girl), Flournoy, who was our Buckwheat, and me. We were close and almost inseparable. We hung together almost every day. The reason we weren't completely inseparable was because of segregation laws in many states, especially in Dixie.

One particular day we were all sitting under three big, shady pecan trees and pondering things to do. We settled on going to see Gene Autry's latest movie and the new serial that was starting at Mr. Otis Boyles' picture show.

We were all excited about our plan until we remembered that Flournoy would either have to go back to his house in colored town or sit in the balcony of the theater all by himself. That wouldn't work.

That's when our mental wheels began to grind out some ideas. The light bulbs in our collective minds came on all at once. We hit upon a plan. We would disguise Flournoy and sneak him into the Gene Autry picture show as my cousin.

Since we were in my yard, under my shade tree, I appointed myself to be Flournoy's haberdasher for the day. I ran into my house and emerged with the right stuff, thanks to my daddy's closet. We got Flournoy a hat, dark glasses, and a much too big, long sport coat for the disguise.

Since Doll Baby was the bossy one, she took over getting Flournoy dressed. Once she was finished, we all clapped to applaud the great disguise. We headed for Mr. Boyles' picture show with my cousin (who really did look different) in tow.

Once we arrived at the theater and after looking at the long line, we decided to sneak Flournoy in through the side exit door of the theater. Once we were inside, settled into our seats with one extra for our friend, and the lights went out, I sneaked over and opened the exit door to let Flournoy in. It worked! No one said a word. We were home free!

While the previews were rolling and after everyone had bought the required Sugar Daddy candy on a stick, a big Coke in a cup for dipping the Sugar Daddy candy sticks, and a large box of popcorn, we had a visitor: Mr. Boyles.

I almost swallowed my Sugar Daddy.

Johnny dropped his popcorn.

Mr. Boyles, who was a big man, leaned down to my level and looked directly into my eyes. I almost died from fright.

Mr. Boyles said in his deep, raspy, drawling whisper, "Sambo. Who's your friend there?"

Scared to death, I immediately said, "My cousin from Philadelphia, the one in Mississippi, not the one in Pennsylvania."

Mr. Boyles sort of smiled and said, "Tell your cousin I hope he likes the picture show, and welcome to Louisville."

As he left, Mr. Boyles tapped my Philadelphia cousin and me on our heads.

We enjoyed the Sugar Daddies, the popcorn, the Cokes, and the movie—twice.

History was made, and we didn't even know it, thanks to Mr. Boyles!

The Cloakroom Caper

When I was in the fourth grade, my mama always made me a big lunch. I rarely knew everything she would pack, but I did know two things. One, it would be delicious, and two, a tasty surprise was always inside that brown paper bag.

My teacher, Miss Murphy, had a preferred form of discipline. She sent you to the cloakroom if you misbehaved in her classroom. Schools today don't have cloakrooms, but back in New Albany, Mississippi, in the 1950s, the cloakroom was like a large windowless closet in the back of the classroom where pupils would hang their coats and hats and stash their lunch sacks.

In fourth grade, I got sent to the cloakroom fifty-two days in a row, which was a school record. Finally, Miss Murphy decided to take action. With a scowly face, she said, "Come with me, young man. We are going to the principal's office. We've got to do something about you being sent to the cloakroom every day."

I was scared.

Next, she told me, "I've called your mother to seek her advice and help." That remark scared me more than the trip to the principal's office, especially when she told me my mama was coming to the meeting. I sure hoped my daddy wouldn't be there, too.

When Miss Murphy and I walked into the principal's office, my mama was already there. I started to go over and kiss my mama, but I didn't get that far. The principal gave me a mean look and said, "Sit down, Sam, and don't say a word."

Not one word was spoken for a few seconds, which felt like an eternity, and all eyes were on me. I think that was the first time I ever noticed my palms sweating. I didn't know what to do or what to say.

I turned to Mama, "Why are you here?"

She didn't answer me. She looked at Miss Murphy and asked, "Why don't you tell us why we are here?"

My teacher began to describe my antics. "Sam is normally a very good student and usually behaves himself, with one exception. Every morning around 9:30, he will do something absolutely unbelievable. For example, he will get up in class and pull a girl's pigtail or belt out some loud remark. Yesterday, he threw an eraser and hit the blackboard, resulting in his fifty-second trip to the cloakroom."

Before she could go any further, my mama stopped the conversation. Both the principal and Miss Murphy thought she was getting ready to defend her little Sam. Instead, Mama asked, "What time did you say he's acting bad?"

Mis Murphy said, "You can set your clock on 9:30 because that's the moment he goes into action."

Mama laughed and said, "I can tell you exactly what's going on. Every day by 9:30, Sam is starving to death. He's famished, wanting something to eat. Isn't his lunch sack in the cloakroom?"

Miss Murphy nodded.

"When he gets hungry, he wants you to send him to the cloakroom because that's where the food is. I always add two sausage biscuits to his lunch bag for recess to satisfy his hunger because he loves sausage biscuits."

The cloakroom caper mystery was solved.

Nanny Became My Best Friend

My folks built us a neat, cottage-style home next door to my daddy's mother. I called her Nanny, but her name was Minnie Rutledge Owen. I think Nanny called me a pain in her fanny.

Why would a grandmother think that about her grandson? Because I deserved it. She loved me dearly, but my middle name was *Mischievous* by age six or seven.

Since we were next–door neighbors, I often practiced my mischievousness on her. I loved to find ways to fluster Nanny.

On this particular summer afternoon, I was sitting on the edge of Nanny's large fish pond in her side yard. The pond was full of water lilies, aquatic plants, goldfish, and several huge, multicolored fish.

I didn't know what kind of fish they were, but I knew they weren't bluegill, bream, crappie, or bass. Those were the only kinds of fish I cared about. Besides, my kinds of fish were delicious to eat at one of Daddy's popular fish fries.

Suddenly, it hit me. The best idea I had had all day. Let's have a fish fry. I would surprise everyone with a string of beautiful, multicolored fish from Nanny's fish pond.

I got my fishing pole, dug up some worms for bait, and went fishing in my newly discovered fishing hole—Nanny's fish pond.

For some reason, the worms didn't work. These fish didn't even look at my bait. They just kept swimming around doing nothing.

I decided I'd show 'em. I ran to our garage next door and got Daddy's fishnet. It worked. I had those huge, multicolored fish lying in the grass, waiting to be fried and eaten at the fish fry.

When Daddy pulled into our driveway and got out of his car, he was happy to see me. Then he saw my stringer of fish. That happy smile quickly evaporated and turned into an expression of fear and anger.

I heard him say, "Holy Shit!"

Next, I heard Nanny scream, "You little devil. Look what you've done!"

I thought, *Why aren't they glad we're gonna have a fish fry?*

As time passed on, I became best friends with Nanny. She educated me on the new Koi fish swimming in her pond. She also shared her many pearls of wisdom and stories from her vast experiences from a different era. She enthralled me immensely.

But the best part of this wonderful relationship is that we became best friends years later while I was playing football at Ole Miss. We had a ritual every Sunday during football season. She had me come to her house thirty miles away from Oxford in New Albany to relive Saturday's contest. She wanted a play–by–play description of what happened during the game. She would sit on her front porch in her rocking chair and wait for me to arrive.

The minute I drove up, Nanny would break out in a great big smile and say, "Come sit here, honey, while I get us something to drink."

She would always return with a small, sterling silver tray holding a glass of fresh lemonade, a juice glass filled to the brim with brown water (also known as bourbon), and her elegant cigarette holder clasping a long, slender Pall Mall.

After a short chat and a welcoming kiss on the cheek, she'd say, "Alright, sweetheart, tell me about it!"

We often relived the Koi debacle and became hysterical as she told her version of the story.

As I matured, I realized how fortunate I was to have Nanny as my grandmother and dear friend. She was a remarkable, complex, competent woman. She helped found several Presbyterian churches in north Mississippi. She was also deeply involved in creating the small but highly successful Blue Mountain College in Blue Mountain, Mississippi.

Nanny was an accomplished artist, especially with charcoal. She was also one of the best cooks in the whole world. Her fried cabbage and cornbread were to die for. Thank you for the memories, Nanny!

A Sister Called Boowa

When I was born, the happiest person on earth, other than my parents, was my ten-year-old sister, Rosemary Rutledge Owen. From all accounts, Rosemary thought I was her gift from God. As far as I know, I was.

I, along with most people, thought Rosemary was absolutely beautiful. She was five feet and three inches tall, and God had favored her with a perfect figure. Her hair was the color of a penny. That earned her a nickname for life. Everyone called her Rusty, and she loved it. Her copper-colored hair was accentuated by her emerald-green eyes. Yes, sir, she was a beautiful girl, but I didn't know it yet. I was just a baby.

As I grew a little older, I tried to pronounce Rosemary's name, and it just wasn't working. Finally, I gave up and settled on calling her Boowa. That moniker was my nickname for Rosemary, and it lasted until the day she died.

Boowa and I became more than big sister and little brother. We became best friends, most of the time. When I grew to the age of six, I began to feel like I could do as I pleased. That didn't sit well with Boowa or my parents because I started to ignore my sister's requests when she was babysitting me.

I remember one summer evening, Mama asked Rosemary to call me to come home to eat supper. I was playing kick the can with my buddies, and I didn't want to quit. Boowa came to get me and said nicely, "Sam, Mother said it's time for you to come home and eat supper."

I was feeling my oats, and I wasn't ready to eat supper yet. So, I yelled, "Go to hell. I ain't going to eat no supper yet!"

Boowa tried to reason with me to no avail. She went home.

It wasn't three minutes later when I saw Daddy storming down the road. He didn't call out to me. As he got closer, he started pulling his belt out of his belt loops.

I started running toward Daddy yelling, "I was just kidding Boowa and Daddy."

Daddy wasn't kidding me. He tore my butt up with his trusty belt.

Boowa didn't say a thing to me at the supper table because I wasn't there. I'd been sent to my room to ponder my butt whoopin'.

Later that evening I went to see Boowa in her room.

At first she wasn't interested in talking with me. But when I said, "Boowa, I'm sorry. I love you," all was forgiven.

Rosemary left home for Ole Miss in 1947 for her freshman year. She was an immediate hit on campus and became a popular girl. She pledged Phi Mu sorority and was the feature twirler of the Ole Miss Rebel band. Later, she was selected as an Ole Miss Beauty and an Ole Miss Favorite. These are coveted honors for any Ole Miss co-ed.

We were so proud of her. I remember bragging about my pretty sister to all my buddies.

I'll never forget the day that Boowa came home for an impromptu visit with her high school friend, Edd Tate Parker, and his best friend Charlie Conerly, both of whom were famous

Ole Miss football players. Charlie was an All-American and the National Player of the Year. I was starstruck when they entered our house.

During her sophomore year, I was seven years old. Boowa asked me if I would like to come to Ole Miss and spend the night with her. Of course I said, "Heck yeah! When?"

The next weekend, I became the only guy I ever knew who spent the night in Somerville Hall. All I remember is that Boowa and her friends had to hide me during bed check when the house mother came through.

From time to time when tailgating in The Grove, someone will come up to me and ask, "Is it true that you…?"

Boowa and I became much closer during my time at Ole Miss. Her husband decided that he wanted to go back to medical school. Since he had to take a few courses to meet medical school entrance requirements, Boowa and I were united again.

Many years later, my phone rang. It was a friend of my sister's, Mrs. Ann Plyler of Memphis. When I answered my phone, Ann said to me, "Sam, I hate calling you with bad news, but our Rusty is gone."

My response to Ann was short. "That breaks my heart."

The New Albany Flood

In the late 1940s, the United States of America was experiencing an economic explosion following the end of World War II. The prosperity that was sweeping the country found its way to Mississippi and New Albany in particular. My daddy decided that he was going to open an appliance store similar to one he had seen in Memphis, but on a smaller scale to fit New Albany's economic profile. New Albany was tiny compared to Memphis, but as the county seat of Union County, it was a thriving, economic hub in North Mississippi.

Main Street was a bustling place, but on Saturdays New Albany appeared to be as busy as Memphis in the minds of New Albanians. There were never any parking spaces along Main Street or the small side streets running off of it; consequently, people improvised and created many additional parking spaces by parking their cars down the center line of the unusually wide strip of pavement bricks making up Main Street.

New Albany had only one policeman on Saturdays, and he couldn't write parking tickets fast enough for the illegal parkers, so he just quit trying. Thus, until this day in 2024, New Albanians are still parking in the middle of Main Street while the police either look the other way or don't look at all. They just don't give a damn.

With the booming economy churning, America moved to new world prominence, and my daddy's new appliance store was doing a land-office business. It appeared that the Owen

Appliance Center was well on its way to becoming a thriving enterprise. Life was good!

My daddy was extremely happy and proud of his success. New washing machines, refrigerators, and cooking ranges flew out the door. Business was so strong that my daddy had been in discussions with the bank to expand the business to some neighboring towns. It appeared that good fortune was about to tap him on his shoulder and say to him, "Welcome to the big time, Snow. Come on in."

Lord knows he deserved it. He also needed it because the Great Depression had not been kind to him or anyone else in our part of the world, but on that day, life was good for Samuel Walton "Snow" Owen Sr. and his family. "Snow" was my daddy's nickname because he had a thick head of hair that was as white as freshly fallen snow.

One summer afternoon, my daddy was standing outside of the Owen Appliance Center talking to several of his friends when the sky began to fill with roiling, dark clouds. That wasn't uncommon in Mississippi's hot summer months, but these clouds looked different. They looked angry and menacing. Could it be that they were trying to develop into a tornado?

The New Albanians, whose cars had completely filled every inch of parking space in the thriving downtown, were hustling and running to their cars and trucks to hustle home ahead of the weather. For those poor souls whose only form of transportation was a wagon pulled by mules, there would be no good ending to what started out as a beautiful day.

Regardless of the mode of transportation, no one wanted to be caught under the churning, scary-looking, black clouds that were about to dump their loads of rain on New Albany and North Mississippi. This also meant that the meandering, shallow portion of the Tallahatchie River that flowed through New Albany was on the verge of becoming a furious, roiling river. To what degree was up to the good Lord and the amount of water that He dumped on the town. Things didn't look so good.

Today, the Tallahatchie River has become a nationally famous river, mainly because Billy Joe McAllister jumped off one of its bridges. Mississippians were quite familiar with the river because it is one of many major waterways that flow through the state and its key, distinctive, geographic regions. New Albany is located in Mississippi's hill country. No one ever jumped off of the bridge in New Albany because it was too visible to the townspeople and especially to the customers and owner of the Owen Appliance Center at the north end of Main Street. The bridge and the river were extremely close to my daddy's appliance store. My daddy and his buddies would have stopped anyone trying to jump unless it was someone they didn't like. In that case they would probably just say, "Let 'em jump."

Another reason people didn't jump off of the bridge was because the water in the Tallahatchie was extremely shallow at this point along the famous tributary. It wasn't even knee deep. When it rained, the river would swell to a meandering body of somewhat deeper water, but not real deep. It would take a rain of biblical proportions to make the Tallahatchie a roaring, dangerous waterway that could become a menace to our area of Mississippi.

Guess what? Those roiling, black clouds that made everyone leave downtown were filled with water to proportions rarely seen before around these parts. When the rain started and the clouds began dumping their load, some New Albanians wondered if anyone had built an ark. If not, they should have, but now it was too late. It rained and rained and rained for several days. There was no letup. Things weren't looking good.

As if on cue, enter Joe Btfsplk, Al Capp's Li'l Abner character with the black cloud above his head. The Tallahatchie River decided to visit downtown New Albany and the Owen Appliance Center. "Ole Tally" didn't just peek into the place; she made a grand entrance by delivering ten to twelve feet of water into the Owen Appliance Center. She didn't stop there. She went on to visit all of downtown, but she paid special attention to my daddy's business.

It was a sad day. That much water swallowing up a building full of electrical appliances isn't good for the equipment or the business. It wasn't good for anything except devastating a man's life. In those days there was no insurance available for this situation, which meant that my daddy lost everything. As luck would have it, "Snow" Owen went from owning a successful business enterprise to owning a bunch of ruined appliances, a building full of water, and a whole lot of Mississippi mud. Not the kind of mud that tastes so good in a Mississippi Mud pie, but the kind that you can't get off your duck-hunting boots after tromping through a rice field.

In a matter of a few hours, my daddy was broke. Flat out busted. He went from the Big House to the Shit House in one stormy, rain-soaked afternoon. I was too young to really understand what all of this meant, but I could certainly tell it was bad.

After the flood, I recall my mama and daddy having numerous, serious conversations about stuff that would lead to fussing, slamming doors, and discrete crying. I also recall a fifth of Ole Crow appearing near my daddy's lounge chair, something that I hadn't seen before this mess.

There had been no need for that because up until now, things were really happy. Life was good. Heck, I thought life was awesome. I still do.

Sam's Bait Shop and Scrap Iron Co.

During the summer of 1951, Sam's Scrap Iron Company was born. At first, Sam's Scrap Iron Company was nothing more than an eighteen-by-eighteen-foot shed where my daddy stored "stuff." Since he didn't use the shed anymore, I talked him into giving it to me if I could get rid of the "stuff" inside of it. After he quizzed me about my intended use for the building, we shook hands and I was in business.

My first undertaking at my new business headquarters was to paint the name of my company on the outside wall above the entry door. Daddy had already painted the entire outside of the shed a pretty deep green with white trim. All I needed to do was to find some white paint and paint my company's name on it in big, white block letters: Sam's Scrap Iron Co. Since I wasn't a professional painter or printer, I must admit the words of my business sign looked like what they were, homemade, but I didn't view them that way. Those words got the job done, and they looked pretty darn good to me.

Rest assured; I didn't have a business plan for my new venture. I didn't even know what a business plan was. My non-existent business plan was put together in my head, and I started executing it. All I knew was that I would get some of my friends to work for me gathering up scrap iron and other metals. Then I would sell the metal to Mr. Tabor, who owned the local junkyard. I would work out the deal with Mr. Tabor, and he would pay me. Then I would pay my buddies for their labors.

Heck, I figured maybe I could even talk Mr. Tabor into helping me haul the scrap iron to his scrap yard. One thing was for sure. If I didn't ask, I would never know the answer to that question. The worst thing that could happen was for him to say no, but I didn't expect him to do that.

As happens in most small towns in the South, my daddy and Mr. Tabor were real good friends. Consequently, he knew me very well and he really liked me. Actually, most people in Louisville really liked me because I was a polite, friendly, respectful boy. One of the many things I love about the South is that most of the Southerners I know are accommodating or at least they will try to be. Mr. Tabor was no exception.

I decided it was time for me to take my first business trip. I began looking for my daddy. I needed to get him to take me in his pickup truck to see Mr. Tabor. Plus, I needed a ride because it was hot, and pedaling a bike on a 90° Mississippi summer day wasn't any fun at all. I pedaled all around town trying to find my daddy, but I couldn't find him anywhere. He wasn't even at Adcock's Cafe, the local hangout where the town's men gathered daily to talk about bream fishing, crappie fishing, Mississippi politics, and football.

My hometown was almost evenly split between Ole Miss and Mississippi State fans, which led to some real heated discussions at Adcock's Cafe during football season. The Ole Miss rivalry with "Cow College" was and is to this day one of, if not the most, heated rivalries in the entire United States of America. Heck, I knew of some families who wouldn't even let the other school's family members eat at the same table at Thanksgiving just before Saturday's big game. Yep, you guessed it. My family was one of those.

After a long, unsuccessful search for my daddy, I decided to just ride my trusty Schwinn bike over to see if Mr. Tabor could help me out collecting the scrap iron. As I had it figured, if I got the scrap iron collected, and he helped me haul it to his junkyard, we both benefitted. He would get his scrap iron, and we would both make some money. I was confident I could sell him on the idea.

When I arrived at the junkyard on my shiny, black, thin-tired Schwinn with three gears on the handlebar, I was dumbfounded at the size of the place. I had only seen it from the road as my daddy and I rode out of town to go fishing or do something else. Plus, I couldn't see over the hills within the sprawling junkyard. It was huge and impressive if you are into comparing junkyards.

There were old cars, rusted out pickup trucks, hay-balers, hay rakes, death trap refrigerators and freezers, buckets, oil drums, and all the other junk that you could imagine that would occupy space in a junkyard on the outskirts of a small town in rural Mississippi. Plus, Mr. Tabor had the customary pack of "junkyard dogs" roaming all over his "Junkdom."

None of them knew who their daddies were, and after looking at their snarling faces, I didn't want to check out their family trees. No one wanted to get up close and personal with these characters. If anyone ever is inclined to look up the definition of a junkyard dog in Mr. Websters' Dictionary, a picture of one of

Mr. Tabor's dogs will probably be the defining image, no words required. No person in his right mind would want to tangle with these vicious-looking scoundrels, even though Mr. Tabor always said, "Don't worry son. They won't bitecha." I wasn't going to test those dogs to find out if he was telling me the truth.

Everywhere I looked, all I could see was junk covering every square inch over countless acres. I was hoping to add my junk to Mr. Tabor's, but I didn't have any yet. I thought to myself, *Is there any more junk near here for my friends to find for me to sell to Mr. Tabor?* It just didn't seem possible, but I was going to find out.

Finally, I mustered up my courage to ask Mr. Tabor what I needed to do to get into the scrap iron business. I told him my idea about employing my friends to gather up all the scrap iron and other metals. After a while, Mr. Tabor looked at me and said, "Sambo, let me get this straight. You're one heckuva salesman. You've got your friends gathering up your scrap, you've got me hauling it for you, and you get the money. That's what I call a pretty good deal for you. What do you think?"

I said, "Yessir, I thought you would agree with me."

After he fell out laughing, he told me that he would pay me so much per pound of scrap iron, galvanized pipe, and the other metals that were acceptable to him. He warned me that scrap tin was worthless so don't waste his time with it. He then gave me some good tips on how to pay my workers. I followed his advice, and after a few days, the acceptable metals started to show up at my green and white bait shop, also known as my headquarters.

Sam's Scrap Iron Co. was born. Lo and behold, I was in "bidness!"

After several weeks of being in the scrap metal business, I pedaled my bike over to see Mr. Tabor again to tell him how things were going. While we were talking, Mr. Tabor told me he was going to go over to the Mississippi Delta to go bream fishing. As we talked about his upcoming fishing trip, I had an idea. I asked him if he was going to use crickets or roaches for bait. He told me he preferred crickets if there were any available. This was on a Monday.

On Thursday, the day before he was leaving for Tchula and Bee Lake, I showed up at the junkyard with two cricket boxes with 200 crickets in each box. Mr. Tabor was thrilled. He paid me $5.00 for those crickets. He also liked the wooden cricket boxes I had made. The sides were screened, so you could see how many crickets you had. I was ecstatic and so were my cricket catchers, the same little colored friends who had gathered up my scrap iron. We were all happy, and in our minds, RICH.

I jumped on my trusty Schwinn bike and went straight to my green and white business headquarters building. I brought out my can of white paint which was about one-third full. Using my trusty paint brush that was hardened and paint covered (I didn't clean it very well), I changed the name on my green and white headquarters to read *Sam's Scrap Iron Co. and Bait Shop*. Watch out, Wall Street. Mississippi is headed your way!

TB Strikes the Owen Family
Louisville, Mississippi 1952

Things were difficult in the Owen household during the summer of 1952. One day Daddy and I were wading among the crazy chickens in one of our chicken houses when he began to cough. At first, his cough didn't sound any different than any other cough, but it got worse and worse. Then it became a violent cough. He couldn't quit or catch his breath. All of a sudden, he started coughing up blood. Not a little blood, but a gusher. I was scared he might die and didn't know what to do. Daddy had become seriously ill.

His best friend and doctor, Bernard Hickman, was having a difficult time pinpointing the diagnosis. Maybe that was because he didn't want to tell my parents that he suspected Daddy had tuberculosis, more commonly called TB. Unfortunately, all things pointed toward that feared diagnosis.

Finally, Dr. Hickman came to our house one evening and sat down with my folks. The first words out of his mouth were, "Corinne, would you please fix Snow and me a stiff drink of bourbon and branch water?" That was the preferred drink for both Dr. Hickman and my daddy. Lots of bourbon, a little ice, and a splash of branch water were the perfect combination. Dr. Hickman and my daddy took the drinks in long, soothing gulps. They didn't sip on their cocktails because the bearer of bad news was about to tell his best friend that he had TB. That was a horrible event because a TB diagnosis immediately dictated that my daddy would be required to be admitted to the Mississippi TB Sanitarium in Whitfield, Mississippi, a small town near Jackson. Even worse was the fact that he would be hospitalized for a long time. That would be a devastating blow to all of us.

The diagnosis also meant that our family's income would be decimated. I didn't know anything about that because Mama protected me. Daddy owned two businesses in Louisville that required his daily attention. He was a general contractor, and he installed, repaired, and maintained air conditioning systems for commercial customers. Air conditioning was a relatively new phenomenon. Because of that, he was an early learner on how to transport freon gas through piping systems that cooled large buildings. That knowledge regarding the transport of freon gas would prove to be a valuable asset later in life when he took a good job as a pipe fitter. But right now, the only thing visible in his future was the uncertainty of a dreaded disease.

The other business that he owned was a chicken farm. What exactly is a chicken farm? A chicken farm translates to a lot of work and a lot of volatility in the market. The chicken business back then wasn't like a chicken yard by an old barn with a bunch of chickens milling around, scratching and pecking out their sustenance from the dirt. Neither was it a business for the faint of heart. If the market was good, lots of money was made. If the market was bad, lots of money was lost.

The chicken farm that my daddy owned consisted of six huge chicken houses that housed 10,000 White Rock fryers in each house. That's a whole bunch of chickens. These chickens didn't lay eggs. They laid something else (the by-product resulting from eating tons of corn mash chicken feed and thousands of gallons of water). These crazy birds were the chickens that made Sunday dinners so spectacular in the South when served with biscuits, gravy, mashed potatoes, and home-grown vegetables. Nope, the stuff that these chickens laid wasn't used to make chicken salad, it was used to make great fertilizer.

These businesses required my daddy's personal attention and presence. No one else in our family could fill in the void that would be created when my daddy left for the TB sanitarium. But at the tender age of ten or eleven, I wasn't aware of the magnitude of the situation, nor was I prepared to take over the businesses. I actually thought that my daddy was going to Jackson to be seen by doctors who specialized in TB and then would return home. Naiveté is a wonderful thing sometimes.

Instead, he was gone for months.

Thank the good Lord, Senator John Stennis, a distant relative of my mama's, heard the news about my daddy's illness. He called Mama to talk about her situation. I had no idea what they were talking about, but whatever it was, it must have been good. Mama was switching back and forth from her fabulous laughs to her sad tears.

What is going on? I asked myself.

When she hung up, she looked at me and said, "God has blessed us, honey! Senator Stennis just told me that I have a job running the local draft board."

I had no idea what a draft board was. I wondered how a board would help us.

Mama recognized my puzzlement so sat me down to explain things to me. She said, "Sam, honey, although this is a good job, it won't pay well enough for us to maintain the standard of living we have enjoyed from the construction and chicken business. She explained to me that our lives were going to change drastically, because we were going to have to watch what we spent and save as much money as we could.

That conversation scared the absolute hell out of me. Somehow, I didn't let on about things, but it signaled to me that I would need to find ways to earn some money.

In reality, this dire situation was a blessing in disguise. I just didn't realize it then. I would later in my life.

I jumped on my Schwinn bicycle to go find a job. My first stop was at the Jitney Jungle Supermarket to talk to Mr. Ben Smith about a job. In those days young boys in small southern towns like Louisville could work bagging groceries and stocking shelves. Nobody cared because it was good for everyone. Mr. Ben gave me a job making twenty-five cents an hour bagging groceries and stocking shelves at his Jitney Jungle.

I started out working on Saturdays only because stores those days were closed on Sundays.

After a couple of weeks of my grocery store career, I realized that this wasn't going to help out very much. I decided that I needed to do something to make more money for Mama.

In the meantime, she would be without the love of her life, and I would be without my best fishing buddy. When would he return? No one knew.

Daddy was away for two whole months with no improvement, and Dr. Hickman was totally perplexed. The treatment he prescribed seemed worthless. Normally it worked, but not this time.

One day, he came by to see Mama about an idea. He said, "Corinne, I just bought a new gadget that may help in treating Snow's illness."

Mama smiled her first real smile in two months. "What's your gimmick, Bernard? You always have something up your sleeve."

Dr. Hickman told her, "I just bought myself a new medical device called a bronchoscope. I'm about to leave for Whitfield to see if it works on Snow. I'll call you as soon as I find out if this thing is as good as they say it is."

I'll never forget the phone call that my mother later received from Dr. Hickman. "Corinne, I had a very successful visit with Snow. The bronchoscopy went exceptionally well."

Mama screamed, "Egads! What did you find out?"

Dr. Hickman responded with a boisterous laugh. "Snow ain't got no TB! I found an abscess in Snow's right lung." He told her, "I stuck that stiff pipe down his lung and pulled out a damn chicken feather. Snow is better already. His days of being hospitalized in the Mississippi TB Sanitarium are over."

I watched as the expression on my mama's face went from stressful concern to sheer joy. Then she asked, "When's he coming home?" She exploded into another round of elation when I heard her say, "You're bringing him home with you? Egads! I'll get the bourbon and branch water ready. We're gonna have a party."

That was one of Mama's happiest moments. Turning to me, she said, "Sweetheart, your daddy's coming home today. Let's get things ready for him. This is the best day of my life."

A Baker's Dozen and a Loaf of Bread: Mississippi Style

I was eleven years old in 1952. As was the case in most small towns in Dixie, life was quite simple for eleven-year-old boys. We rode our bikes everywhere. The fire and tornado sirens went off every day at noon to signal us to go home for dinner. Remember, in those days in the South, dinner was the noon meal.

Everybody in Louisville would drop what they were doing and go to dinner. Some went home. Some went to cafes. Some went to drive-ins with carhops and trays hooked onto partially rolled-down windows. Some found the shade of a big oak tree to serve as nature's dining room.

After dinner, my buddies and I went bream fishing at one of the many lakes within a reasonable bike ride from downtown. We were outfitted with limber cane poles and cricket boxes full of crickets, the best bream bait that ever existed.

We didn't need any fancy fishing equipment because the stuff we had suited us just fine. Poles were preferable because bream liked to hang out in places where they have cover, which makes casting impossible. The trusty cane pole was the perfect equipment for reaching otherwise unreachable places where bream tend to hang out and bed.

We played follow the leader on our bikes. We did the usual jumps and crazy stunts to outdo one another. Sometimes we were successful, but most often the followers were up to the task. Then one would take over the leadership role until replaced by the next one.

We often rode by Baker's Bakery. When the fresh bread was baking in the ovens, and the best donuts ever made were cooking in smoldering oil, the aroma was beyond tempting. Those are two of the reasons why Baker's Bakery was such a special place to us.

It was as if we were Jason and the Argonauts under the spell of the fresh, baking bread's aroma instead of the mythical Sirens. The name of the bakery was coincidental because Mr. Baker owned the place. He was also one of the nicest men who ever walked on Mississippi dirt. He was generous, too.

We would ride up to the rather small bakery and go into the kitchen through the screened back door. Mr. Baker loved seeing us come into his Holy Temple, his kitchen. It was as clean as a pin, but no person on earth can keep flour from making its presence known.

Mr. Baker loved hearing the same greeting every time we walked through the door. I always said, "Hi, Mr. Baker. Got any samples we need to check out for you today?"

The donut sampling scheme was my idea, and it worked every time. Mr. Baker's response was always the same. He would flash us a big grin and say, "Go over yonder and look on that cooling rack to see if there is anything there that needs sampling."

Sure enough, there would always be several big, round, honey-colored donuts ready for testing. They were covered with a smooth, sugary, and almost invisible glaze that drizzled down the sides of each one onto the sheet pan where they cooled.

They just begged us to eat them.

Sure enough, Mr. Baker would then ask, "Did you find any?"

I would say, "Yessiree. There's a lot of 'em."

Mr. Baker would then come through as always, "Take one and let me know if they're fit to be sold."

This same ritual occurred two or three times a month, and the answer was always the same, "Yessir Mr. Baker, these are okay to be sold." Followed by, "These may be the best donuts you ever made."

With that declaration, we would each get a bag with a "Baker's Dozen" of donuts in them to take home to our mamas. Of course, we would always ask Mr. Baker to just charge it to our mamas' accounts, which he gladly did.

Oh yeah, I almost forgot, we would also take a loaf of his fabulous bread because our mamas had figured Mr. Baker's bread was every bit as good as theirs and made their lives a whole lot easier. This nice gesture by Mr. Baker did not come without reciprocation.

Whenever I went bream fishing, which was frequently in the spring and summer, I would always take Mr. Baker a mess of big, copper-nosed bluegills, fully cleaned and dressed.

That was the way life worked in the little towns and hamlets throughout Mississippi. Thank God I was exposed to that aspect of life because I was taught early to share my blessings with the people I love.

Sam Meets Billy Graham
Jackson, Mississippi, 1952

As a young man growing up in a small Mississippi town, one of the most important things in my life was participating in church. My folks weren't fanatics or religious zealots, but they made it quite clear that I was going to have God in my life. I went to Sunday school most Sundays, even if my folks didn't go. My daddy had a habit of calling the lake his church, and many times I often went to his church with him and a congregation of crickets.

On the other hand, the Presbyterian Church doors couldn't open without my grandmother being there. She wanted me to be a preacher after I finished playing football and graduated from Ole Miss. The Ole Miss football player part was certainly fine with me, but I wasn't sure about the preacher part of that equation. Heck, I was only eleven years old, but my grandmother had this dream. She was certain that I would be a good football player, but she was convinced that I would be the next Peter Marshall. Only half of her dream came true; I became an Ole Miss football player. My Peter Marshall imitation didn't materialize. At least not in a pulpit.

I was no different from the other children my age. I grumbled and groused about always having to go to Sunday School, prayer meetings, and church outings. I preferred to go fishing with my daddy. I did that a lot. I had inherited his belief that a bream lake was a glorious cathedral where God had done some of his finest work by creating those beautiful, copper-nosed bluegills. We would sit by the sleepy oxbow lake filled with beautiful fish, surrounded by majestic cypress trees and wispy Spanish moss draping the gnarly limbs and branches. Sometimes the moss shared the trees with snakes that dangled from the branches.

Nothing is more soothing than watching rustling gray moss shimmer in the breeze while sitting in a jon boat and catching big bream that are thick and wide. Nothing is worse than having one of those snakes fall out of the tree into the boat and be scared to death while snakes and humans scramble to get away from each other. Most of the time, we won and snakes lost. On occasion, the snake won when we fell out of the boat.

I began to realize that through my participation in the activities of the First Presbyterian Church of Louisville, Mississippi, I had a blessed life. I had fun with all of my friends and met some cute girls. Now that made it worthwhile. It finally dawned on me that if I didn't participate in those churchy things, I would be all alone in my life because all of my friends were participating under the same set of rules and circumstances that I had. I believe it was a conspiracy that all of the parents concocted. Regardless, the parents won out like they always did. I begrudgingly did what was expected of me, but I never admitted when I actually enjoyed it.

The most rewarding thing about being involved with the church is that it made me feel peaceful. It made me feel happy. It made me want to do good deeds for others. I also realized doing kind things for others was fun. That is a trait that is central to my character to this day. Yep, I do enjoy helping other people. I believe that I read that somewhere else. Oh yeah, now I remember. It's known as The Golden Rule: "Do unto others as you would have them do unto you."

Our youth leader at the church was an unbelievable young woman. Her name was Charlotte Rose. She was about twenty-five to thirty years old. She was absolutely beautiful. Her face and features were stunning, but her heart and soul were even more exquisite. Unfortunately, Miss Rose had been stricken by polio during the epidemic. She was crippled and needed crutches to walk. We were sad for her at first, but once we really got to know her, we didn't even see her crutches anymore. She was an awesome lady who possessed an air about her that personified serenity.

One day she told us that she had an announcement to make. She proceeded to tell us that she was going to be married, and she wanted all of us to come to her wedding. My heart sank. I felt as if I had been hit in the stomach with a baseball bat. I was destroyed because I loved Miss Rose, and I thought she loved me. Miss Rose sensed that I was sad, and she took me aside to explain her love for me, my love toward her, and her love for her future husband. I was relieved after receiving her gentle guidance, and I enjoyed learning that we had all "won" because of this experience. Miss Rose explained that God had guided us through our relationships and we were better for it.

I am convinced that her beautiful presence and her unbelievable, positive attitude subconsciously influenced me throughout my life. I was born with my own positive, happy personality, and hers strengthened mine. After Miss Rose was married, she and her new husband moved away from Louisville. I lost track of her. I never saw her again, but her impact on my life is still with me to this day. I didn't lose my memories of her and what she taught me at First Presbyterian Church of Louisville, Mississippi. Miss Rose was just one of the many gifts that He has given me throughout my life.

During one of our Sunday School lessons, Miss Rose had us enthralled with her story about a man who was changing the world in an extremely positive way. She told us that this man was a special man of God who had a charismatic relationship with the people that was similar to the relationship that Jesus had when he was changing the world. Of course, we listened to her comments with skepticism. We made jokes about the new Jesus behind Miss Rose's back. I am not sure if she knew what we were doing, but she never faltered. She just kept on talking about Reverend Billy Graham and the impact that he was making on the world. Of course, we never faltered either. We kept on making jokes about how Reverend Billy could heal our favorite Ole Miss football player if he got hurt, or how he could help us find huge bream beds so we could fill our jon boats with fishes and feed the multitudes. Of course, if Miss Rose had ever heard us acting like that, she would have admonished us about our behavior. She would never raise her voice or her hand. She would just look at us with serenity and disappointment in her face. That combination alone would make us regret our behavior, embarrass us, and make us want to grovel on the floor.

A couple of weeks later during Sunday School, Miss Rose told us that Reverend Billy Graham was taking his Crusade for Christ on a major tour across the United States. Then Miss Rose announced that Reverend Graham was bringing his crusade to Jackson, Mississippi, and we were going to attend. She had received approval to take two yellow school buses to the Billy Graham Crusade. Typically, I raised my hand and Miss Rose called on me. I made some comment that brought a roar of laughter from the entire class. Miss Rose maintained her composure and suppressed the urge to laugh as she scolded me for being disruptive.

Miss Rose truly adored me. She met with my parents on several occasions to try to persuade them to encourage me to become a minister. She told my mama and daddy what she had told me many times, that I was a leader of men. She told my parents that I could become another Billy Graham if I would commit to it. She went on to elaborate that I had a wonderful heart with the ability to lead large groups of people.

Miss Rose asked my folks for their permission for me to go to Jackson to hear Reverend Billy Graham; furthermore, she was going to ensure that I *met* him. Of course, my folks gave her their blessings. After that meeting, my mama and daddy met with me, they told me about their talk with Miss Rose, and they asked me what I thought about Miss Rose's plan. I told them that I would like to meet Reverend Graham.

Two days later we boarded the yellow school buses for our two-and-a-half-hour road trip to the high school stadium near Jackson, where the Billy Graham Crusade was being held. Of course, my mama had made me a lunch to tide me over if I got hungry. Typically, my mama had filled a shoe box lunch with fried chicken, her fabulous biscuits, potato salad, deviled eggs, pimento cheese sandwiches, and a big slice of pound cake with a sad streak running through it. She had also filled a thermos bottle with iced tea, lemon, a little pineapple juice, and sugar.

Heck, I didn't care about the crusade as long as I had my shoe box lunch. It was worth a two-and-one-half-hour road trip in an old yellow school bus with awful seats to get one of my mother's famous box lunches. I hadn't been on the bus ten minutes before I was into the shoe box lunch and hunting for one of those plump fried thighs and a biscuit. There has never been a morsel of food on this planet that tastes better than my mama's fried chicken and biscuits. Then I thought, *Should I eat one of the pimento cheese sandwiches first?* I decided to alternate bites, but the fried chicken thigh won first place. This moment in time was Heaven on earth. Then the pimento cheese made it all come together to produce some of the best flavors known to man.

Finally, our yellow chariots arrived at the stadium where the Billy Graham Crusade was to take place. I had no idea what to expect. I had never been to a religious rally before. When we got off the bus, I was shocked. I had never seen a crowd this big except at an Ole Miss football game. I couldn't believe that this many people were here to listen to a preacher from North Carolina. The multitude was here. I wondered why. What did this fellow have that our preacher at First Presbyterian Church in Louisville didn't have?

We entered the stadium, and Miss Rose came up to me and took me by the arm and said to come with her. She guided me to our seats near the podium where Reverend Graham would preach. There was a gentleman standing by the podium, and he saw Miss Rose. It was obvious that he recognized her as he came over to her and gave her a big, friendly hug. Then he looked at me and asked if I was the young man she had told him about. She beamed her beautiful smile and nodded, "Yes." He then looked at me and told me that he would see me immediately following the service. He introduced himself as Mr. George Beverly Shea.

I asked Miss Rose who Mr. Shea was and what his job was. She told me to be patient and I would know real soon. About then the music started, and Mr. Shea began singing the old-time favorites with a booming, beautiful voice. The melodies engulfed the soul of the crowd and created an atmosphere that cast a calm spell throughout the balmy Mississippi night. I had never experienced anything like this in my life. My mood was serene. After several fabulous hymns, Mr. Shea left the podium. That is when Reverend Billy Graham walked up to the podium. He was an impressive figure with an aura about him that projected confidence, warmth, and determination. Yes, he just looked different. Then I recalled what Miss Rose had told us about

Reverend Graham. She had told us that he had a charismatic presence about him that resonates with the multitudes. When he began to speak to the audience that had filled the stadium seats and the chairs that covered the entire football field, I understood what Miss Rose had said about him. He was captivating. I literally felt like he was talking directly to me. His face was radiant and projected a sense of authority that was shrouded in humility. I was enthralled and liked how I felt. I was hooked, and I am still glad that I was.

Mr. Graham began his sermon with several wonderful stories. He then delivered the most beautiful and moving sermon I had ever heard. He didn't scream. He didn't yell. He didn't emote. He enveloped us. His words filled my heart and soul with a warmth that I had never experienced before. What was happening to me? After Reverend Graham completed his sermon, he invited the audience to come forward and meet one of his associates and accept Jesus Christ as their Lord and Savior. I was in awe when I witnessed more than half of those in attendance get out of their seats and move forward. I was one of those people.

When I started toward the place where I was supposed to go, I noticed that Miss Rose was smiling and crying at the same time. I took her hand and thanked her for bringing me to the Billy Graham Crusade. As I walked onto the field to meet one of the associates, I was intercepted by George Beverly Shea. He took me by the arm and led me to Reverend Graham and introduced us. I was awestruck. He perceived that and made me relax with a warm smile and hug. Then Mr. Shea led me to one of the tents where people were gathering to accept Jesus Christ as their Lord and Savior. He led me to a small table with two chairs and invited me to have a seat. He then looked me in the eye and said that Charlotte Rose hoped that I would do what I was doing. He then told me that she had told him that I was a leader of men and would one day change my part of the world. I was stunned. He then took my hand and asked me if I accepted Jesus as my Lord and Savior? I told him that I did.

On the bus ride back to Louisville, I had a different feeling in my heart and soul than I had on the way to the crusade. It was difficult to explain. Going to the Crusade, the only thing on my mind was my box lunch. Now I had different food for thought.

I had a serene, wonderful aura about me. I saw things differently than I had before. I had always gone to Sunday School and church. I had heard many sermons, but I had never heard a sermon like the one that I heard that night. Billy Graham changed me. He delivered a message that resonated with me. He made me feel different. He made me realize that Jesus was the answer to my questions, the beam of light in darkness, and the foundation of life.

I will never forget that time in my life and where it took me. Although many years have come and gone since my encounter with Billy Graham, I have always tried my best to keep Jesus Christ first in my heart, life, and soul. For the most part I have succeeded, but I have also been a typical human being and strayed from the path. Now that I am in the twilight of my life, I am making a sincere effort to improve my relationship with Jesus. It's always time!

The Holy Rollers Come to Town

Aunt Bess noticed a whole bunch of activity going on over on the huge, vacant lot a couple of blocks from the spot where the lemonade party was taking place. She didn't know what was going on even though she, her sisters, and brothers owned the property. She was puzzled.

In small towns in the Deep South like Louisville, any kind of activity that deviates from the everyday norm is big news. The news spreads all over town in no time flat. It would be discussed in every cafe, drugstore, soda fountain, dress shop, feed store, and gossip heaven: the barbershop. In the blink of an eye, everyone knew the distorted story.

Bess, Vergie, and the boys watched with great inquisitiveness all of the activity going on down the street. All of a sudden, I jumped up and yelled to my buddies, "Come on, let's go see what's going on!"

Off we went lickety-split.

When I got to the lot, the activity had accelerated and there were several men and women going about the business of unloading chairs, tents, poles, lights, and something that looked like a pulpit from a church. It was crazy.

Nobody talked much. They were a solemn bunch. Most of them were dressed in black. What words were spoken, we couldn't understand. They weren't talking or yelling. They were just busy at what they were doing and jabbering to each other.

I walked over to one of the rather oddly acting characters erecting the tent and asked, "Are y'all from the circus? You know from time to time the Clyde Beatty Circus comes through here. They always put their tent up on this lot. My mama and her brothers and sisters own it. They got it when my granddaddy died. I bet y'all are with the Clyde Beatty Circus, aren't you? Can my buddies and I help you put up your tent for free passes to the circus?"

Nobody answered. They just pointed to a person who looked like Ichabod Crane. He was tall and lanky. He wore a tall black hat and was dressed all in black. I timidly went over to the strange-looking fellow and posed the same question about circus tickets.

That exchange must have struck a nerve. The odd-looking man appeared agitated and said, "We ain't with no circus. We're here to have a tent revival to praise the Lord. It starts tonight. We're gonna have a lot of folks start coming in here this afternoon. You coming?"

I asked him, "What time will y'all start?"

The tent erectors turned to look at each other and then turned to look at the peculiar looking character to hear his answer.

I thought to myself, *This fella looks just like one of those guys in a scary Dracula movie who is dressed up in a tall, black hat and black suit with tails and drives a hearse drawn by black horses.*

The gang and I didn't ever see much more than that in those movies because we always pulled our jackets or shirts over our heads to hide from any monsters that might be lurking around in the theater.

After a few minutes, the weird-looking man stuck out his bony hand. His long, skinny fingers were scary. His Adam's apple stuck out really far, and it bounced up and down when he talked. I couldn't make myself touch his scary looking hand. I ran to my Schwinn.

I led the gang to a quiet place where we could discuss an idea that hit me as I was talking to that creepy man. I began describing my idea to the gang. They were all ears, listened intently, and nodded their heads in excited agreement with what I had to say. The plan was made.

The Tent Revival Was a Real Blowout

Just as the dusky light of evening began to cover Louisville in a peaceful glow, the multitude of revival goers began arriving in old cars and trucks, mule-drawn wagons, and a few tractors. The tent revival was officially underway. The organ was belting out everybody's favorite hymns. As the organ played, the weird-looking tall man, wearing a top hat and black tails, stood in vigilance.

After the tent was packed with holy rollers, the head holy roller, the Ichabod Crane-looking character, took to the pulpit. He began his fire and brimstone preaching. The more he ranted and raved, the more the crowd became raptured.

People were cheering, many speaking in a language I had never heard at the First Presbyterian Church of Louisville. They were flailing their hands. Several were rolling around in the sawdust that had been spread on the ground.

The gang was mesmerized as we watched. We had never seen anything like this in our lives. Ichabod hadn't seen us sidle up on our trusty Schwinns.

The place was rocking. Rapture was rapturing. The evening was now at a crescendo.

Suddenly, a light in the top of the tent was turned on. Ichabod began climbing the center tent pole toward the bright light that represented Heaven.

As he would almost reach the bright, white light, the light would turn red and Ichabod would slide down the pole a bit toward Hell as he shouted, "The Devil's got me by my coattails. He's yanking me into the fiery pits of Hell." The place then turned into bedlam.

That was the cue for the gang to have its own rapture. The plan that I had dreamed up was implemented at the perfect moment of rapture.

I lit the first cherry bomb and threw it among the holy rollers wallowing around in the sawdust. My stunt was closely followed by Lance, Johnny, Flournoy, and Doll Baby lighting blockbusters and cherry bombs. They, too, threw theirs where I threw mine. On target!

When the first explosion went off, Ichabod fell from Heaven into the sawdust of Hades. The subsequent explosions sent the holy rollers scurrying, running, and screaming to their wagons, cars, and trucks. Ichabod was trying to get his breath back. The revival was over.

The Devil made us do it, but it was my idea.

The gang jumped onto our trusty bikes and pedaled as fast as we could to our special place to congratulate each other. Then we pedaled home as fast as we could. As I entered my house, Mama and Daddy asked me, "What did y'all do this evening?"

"We went to the tent revival." I kissed them goodnight and went to bed smiling.

My Dog Named Dawg

My lifelong dream as a young boy was to play football for my beloved Ole Miss Rebels. In my daydreams the Rebels were always playing in the closing seconds of an imaginary Rose Bowl game, the granddaddy of all bowls. Notre Dame went down 7-0. Next was Southern Cal 21-20. Then, the Wolverines were bagged 35-28 and so on. It didn't matter who the opponent was, my Rebels always won. Oh yeah, *yours truly* always scored the winning touchdown as the horn went off to end the game.

To prove my point about my love for Ole Miss, I'll share this special story. In 1948 I was seven years old and living in my hometown of New Albany, Mississippi. I was walking alone and headed for home late one glorious autumn afternoon. I had just finished a hard-fought neighborhood football game with the Fighting Irish of Notre Dame. Predictably, the Rebels won. We beat the Fighting Irish in the Rose Bowl as I ran a punt back eighty-nine yards to score the game winner as the horn went off. The crowd went crazy! So did I.

As I was sauntering along, savoring the sweet taste of victory, I heard a strange, whimpering sound. It was an odd, distressful sound. I stopped to try to determine what I was hearing and where the noise was coming from. That's when I saw a shivering, scared, little dog all curled up next to the base of a fire plug. That's what we called a fire hydrant in 1948 Mississippi. I still do.

I approached the pitiful little creature carefully because we had heard reports of a *mad dog* with rabies in and around New

Albany. I didn't know what was wrong with this dog, but I wasn't gonna let her bite me. I had been told by my folks that if a rabid dog bit me, they would stick a big needle in my stomach every day for 21 days to shoot me full of rabies medicine that was thick like buttermilk and painful beyond belief. NO WAY! That's why I was being so careful.

After observing the scared little creature for several minutes, I realized what was wrong with her. This wasn't a mad dog. It was a soon-to-be mama dog about to give birth to a litter of cur puppies. The small, defenseless, future mama was shivering and whimpering, displaying the saddest pair of eyes I had ever seen. Those eyes accentuated her stressful plight. They also captured my heart. Being the eternal optimist that I am, I was convinced that God had brought me this dog. From that day forth she would answer to her new name, Dawg.

I decided to carry Dawg in my arms to my house about a half a block away. There she could have her babies with the help of my mama. Help she needed and help she got as she started giving birth to seven little puppies later that night. During the entire ordeal, my daddy kept telling me, "We aren't keeping these damn cur dogs in this house." I heard him, but I didn't listen because we (the dogs and I) had Mama on our side. I realized that I would have to appeal to my sweet mama to help me change Daddy's mind. I knew she could do that. She did. It worked. They stayed.

Since God had brought these puppies into my life, it was imperative for me to give them appropriate names. I didn't select Matthew, Mark, Luke, or John as names, though. I decided to name them Jimmy, Buster, Barney, Showboat, Kayo, Charlie, and Tank after my favorite Ole Miss football players, regardless of their sex. They were Rebels now. That is true love. It worked. They stayed.

Mama did her thing as usual. Sure enough, Daddy agreed to let me keep all of the puppies until I got tired of fiddling with them, which didn't take long. We found a home for all of the puppies among the people who lived on my great uncle Kinloch's farm. I kept Dawg with me because I loved her so much.

Vergie and the Haints' Haint

Throughout my young life in Mississippi, I heard many stories and tales about haints. Unfortunately, I don't remember all of those fabulous stories, but I do remember my favorite storytellers sitting in the kitchen, shelling peas and butterbeans, laughing and talking. These are great memories of a time gone by. I would sit with Vergie, Elsie, Angie, Elouise, and Mammy for hours at a time, mesmerized by their stories. Those wonderful ladies, all my second mamas, were the help in our family.

This story is my favorite haint story for two reasons. First, it really happened when I was a young boy. Secondly, it was told to me by my favorite compadre, Vergie, my breakfast-eating friend. Vergie's version of this story is better than this typewritten one because her facial expressions, her hand gestures, and her voice inflections were priceless. She literally reminded me of Prissy in *Gone with the Wind*. Let's just refer to this Vergie story as *Vergie and The Haints' Haint*. Here it is.

It was a typical summer Saturday night in Louisville. The night was hot and sultry, but bearable. All of the stores and shops on Main Street were open till 9:30 p.m., so Saturday nights in Louisville were much fun in those days. Although segregation laws were in effect throughout the South, not just Mississippi, they were somewhat overlooked on Saturday nights in Louisville, Mississippi. I reckon that's because money flowed and its color was green. The truth of the matter is money has no social status.

It's merely a medium of exchange, and on Saturday nights money was exchanging and flowing.

The atmosphere was electric, fun, and festive. Music was blaring over loudspeakers to help with the cakewalks, one for whites and one for coloreds. Once all of the cakes were gone to the lucky contestants, everyone in my hometown would head for their homes.

Of course, the white folks went their way and the colored folks went theirs. There was one fly in the ointment. The colored folks had to pass by the huge, eerie, main cemetery in Louisville. It, too, was for white folks only. The colored cemetery was in their part of town.

This particular night was a bit different. While everyone was on Main Street enjoying the music, the festivities, and the cakewalks, the huge white Russian Wolfhound owned by a new family who had just moved to Louisville got out of its pen. Instead of going to the cakewalks and festivities downtown, the big, snow-white dog, with its pure white, long-haired coat, headed straight for the white cemetery to get away from the strange stuff the humans were doing downtown on Main Street. The frightened dog hid in the cemetery near one of the large, ghostly tombstones that reminded me of a gargoyle in a Dracula movie.

Meanwhile, Vergie and her throng of friends were headed home and walking on the sidewalk that took them past this huge, main cemetery. They were always scared to death to walk by the cemetery at night because they didn't want the haints to get them. They approached the cemetery very cautiously just about the same time the Russian Wolfhound found its safe spot to hide on the huge plot guarded by that eerie tombstone.

As usual, Vergie and her crowd were making lots of noise to be sure to scare away any haints that may have been lurking among the tombstones. They weren't aware of the dog. The dog wasn't aware of them. Besides, he was new to Louisville. The dog became more frightened when it heard the clamor emanating from Vergie's crowd as they approached the cemetery. The Russian Wolfhound decided it was time to get the hell out of there. So the huge dog, with its flowing white coat of hair, took off running in fright. As fate would have it, the enormous apparition leaped over the rather high cemetery fence just as Vergie and her crowd reached the point of exit for the frightened dog.

When Vergie's crowd saw the haint soaring in mid-air to escape the terror of the night, they cast down their packages and cakes they had won at the cakewalk. They screamed at the top of their lungs. They ran off in the opposite direction of the frightened Russian Wolfhound. Both the dog and Vergie's crowd ran lickety-split. After the haint's dramatic exit from the cemetery, things changed in Louisville. Vergie and her crowd found a different route to take in the future. As for the Russian Wolfhound, to this day, no one knows what happened to that beautiful dog. It, too, took a different route.

Vergie survived to tell my favorite story to Mama and me at breakfast the following Monday. When she finished with her hilarious tale, our sides were sore from laughing so hard.

The Haints Save the Night

My daddy was devastated after losing the Circuit Court Clerk election in New Albany by just a few votes. He decided to move our family to my mother's hometown of Louisville, to start a new chicken business.

Initially, he started the business by constructing three huge chicken houses. Each house was home to 10,000 Plymouth Rock chickens, the dumbest animals that God ever put on the face of the earth. That adds up to 30,000 snow white, stupid chickens that only live to eat, crap, cackle, and taste good once brined and fried to a crispy taste of heaven. There is no food on mother earth that tastes better than properly fried chicken.

With the success of the initial three houses, my daddy decided to expand to double the size of his business. As the number of chickens grew, so did the success of the Owen Chicken Farm. To turn over 60,000 stupid, crazy chickens every six to eight weeks was hard work.

Here's why. It was a hectic frenzy of bedlam as the chickens were cooped, loaded on huge flatbed trucks, and sent to slaughterhouses for Hormel or Swift Packing Companies.

Once the chickens were gone, the process started all over again. First the houses had to be cleaned out by removing several inches of chicken crap and sending it off to fertilizer plants to become the food for garden vegetation. Then the houses had to be sanitized and prepared for the next load of dumb-assed chicks so the process could start all over again.

One summer day Daddy took several of my friends and me to the chicken farm to help him with some chores. The Owen Chicken Farm was located on several acres of land which were part of the huge farm that my mother's daddy had left to her, her two sisters Bess and Halley, and her two brothers Roger and Olen. The farm was between 1,200 and 1,600 acres of crops, pastures, and timber land. It was a typical Mississippi farm that was home to cotton, soybeans, several fabulous fishing lakes, numerous cattle, and lots of fun bird hunts. To me, it was heaven on earth, especially when I could stop by for a country ham biscuit at one of the sharecroppers' houses while bird hunting or bream fishing. The lakes were full of copper-nosed bluegills that were affectionately known as "Titty" Bream. That was the name that my daddy had given the angry, battling fish because they were too big to hold in your hand without pressing them up against your titties.

As we were carrying out the chores that Daddy had assigned us, we noticed that the protective screening that allowed air flow in the chicken houses had been cut open and re-secured to allow easy access to 10,000 dumb-assed chickens. I told Daddy what I had found, and he realized that someone was entering the chicken house and helping himself to some of the finest tasting chickens that man had ever raised. I had detected a chicken thieving operation. There was no way of knowing the scale of this chicken caper, but it was sure to grow if it wasn't stopped immediately.

After talking things over with Roscoe, the farm's overseer, Daddy and Roscoe decided to put a scheme together to stop the chicken rustlers. After much consternation and thought, they decided on a plan that they thought would work.

Daddy had me recruit my buddies to help solve this problem. We had a meeting. Daddy told us about his plan. My friends and I were going to be haints for the night and the saviors of the chicken business. He then told us about the chicken rustlers that he and Roscoe had witnessed stealing our chickens through the opening I had discovered. The chicken rustlers were three pickup truck loads of colored men who were breaking into the houses and taking several crates full of chickens.

We were going to be haints because Negroes were scared to death of haints. They believed the evil spirits would eat the eyes right out of their heads. So, Daddy handed each of us a sheet that had a ball in the middle, stuffed in there like a head. Tied around that head was a piece of light rope to allow the sheet to dangle and to be jerked up and down as if it were flying, floating, and levitating, all at the same time. He told us that, on his cue, our job was to moan loudly and scream as we jiggled our haints up and down.

We were now ready to do our thing. As the evening turned into darkness, Daddy and Roscoe helped each of us get into the trees near the chicken houses. Once situated, all we had to do was wait in silence, but that's not an easy task for a bunch of ten-year-old boys. After a while and just before the fidgeting started, we heard some laughing and jabbering emanating from three pickup trucks full of chicken rustlers.

They stopped, unloaded the trucks, and were about to take off into the chicken houses when Daddy and Roscoe opened fire into the air with their shotguns to signal the haints. We screamed and moaned and jiggled our sheets.

All at once, the chicken rustlers dropped their chicken coops, tossed their gear, left their trucks running, and ran off into the night, never to be seen again.

Unfortunately for them, the sheriff was able to trace the truck tags back to the perpetrators. The chicken rustlers would be plucking chickens at Parchman Farm Prison on the Mississippi Delta.

Hey, convict, pass the chicken please.

Daddy told us, "Thank you haints. Y'all saved the night!"

For the Sake of My Family

In the late 1940s, my family and I were living in Louisville, Mississippi, my mama's hometown. Louisville was a fun place to live. Mama and Daddy knew I was happy and enjoyed being there.

To me, Louisville was a party town. My folks and all their friends were always looking for a reason to grill steaks or to have fabulous fish fries at our house or at Aunt Bess' house, which was next door.

Regardless of the reason for the party, there was one person in town who was essential to every party's success. He may not be an invited guest, but he would provide the most critical element of the party. That person was Shot Eubanks.

Shot was the owner of the most popular used car lot in that part of Mississippi. The lot was located on the western edge of town on a plot of unkempt land. The remarkable thing about the car lot was that it had only four dilapidated cars lying in rather tall Johnson grass and weeds. Those cars were on the verge of becoming scrap metal, but they weren't going anywhere because they served a crucial purpose for the citizens of Louisville. Those four vehicles stored Shot's actual business wares.

The old Studebaker Coupe was full of pints and fifths of Old Crow Bourbon. The huge, four-door Packard housed the Cutty Sark Scotch Whisky. The Ford sedan was the home of vodka and gin. The Chevy panel truck housed cases of beer and tequila.

Shot's used car lot wasn't big, but it was extremely popular to almost every adult living in Louisville and surrounding counties.

Because of Shot's popularity, it was now time for the periodic election to determine whether or not Louisville and Winston County would become wet or dry. Wet meant that the sale of alcohol was legal. Dry meant the opposite. Mississippi and Louisville in particular had always been dry. Shot wanted to keep it that way. When the governing bodies of Louisville and Winston County declared there would be a referendum to determine whether or not liquor and beer sales would be legalized, all hell broke loose.

Of course, the largest religious group in Louisville, the Southern Baptists, went into action to defeat the sale of alcohol in any form. That was ironic, since the members of the pious Baptist church and their deacons were Shot's best customers. (They just didn't want anyone to know it.)

My Uncle Roy Lancaster was their king since he was the head deacon of the huge First Baptist Church congregation. He never missed the Wednesday night prayer meetings. He also never missed having a few belts of bourbon with some of his deacon buddies after those weekly prayer meetings.

After much deliberation and discussion, the Baptists decided that they would provide bumper stickers to the citizens of Louisville and Winston County to defeat the legalization referendum allowing the sale of alcohol. The Baptist bumper sticker read:

FOR THE SAKE OF YOUR FAMILY VOTE DRY!

Shot never attended any Baptist worship services or any other church services that I'm aware of, but he did immensely appreciate the Baptists' stance against legalizing the sale of alcohol. Consequently, Shot decided to join forces with the Baptists to defeat the referendum. He had only one bumper sticker made to put on the bumper of his Ford pickup truck. Shot's bumper sticker read:

FOR THE SAKE OF MY FAMILY VOTE DRY!

The election was held. The votes were cast. The Baptists won. Ironically, so did Louisville's only bootlegger. Shot's life went on.

Ironically, Shot Eubanks remained in the bootlegging business for a long time. Bootlegging became a thing of the past in 1966 when the State of Mississippi voted to allow each county to decide by referendum whether or not to allow alcohol sales. There are places where alcohol sales are still illegal. Those places are few and far between because Mississippians are party animals.

The Pants: A Dream Comes True

I was six years old and living in Louisville, Mississippi. The year was 1947. Charley Conerly had returned to Ole Miss to play football for the Rebels after World War II. He had entered Ole Miss in 1942 but left to serve as a U.S. Marine in the South Pacific during the war, where he fought in the Battle of Guam. He returned to Ole Miss in 1946 and led the Rebels to their first SEC Championship in 1947. During that season, he led the nation in pass completions, was voted a consensus All-American, and was named National Player of the Year. Needless to say, he was a hero to almost every young Mississippi boy, especially to me because he was a good friend of my sister, Rosemary "Rusty" Rutledge Owen. Remember, Rusty was the feature twirling majorette for the Ole Miss Rebel Band.

Although my sister was special to me, Charley Conerly was my hero. He once gave me his Ole Miss jersey, #42, after a game. From then on, I dreamed of playing quarterback for Ole Miss and wearing #42.

That year I asked Santa Claus to bring me some Ole Miss football pants for Christmas to go with my Ole Miss jersey that #42 had given me. Thank the Lord, Santa came through.

I vividly remember my mama telling me on Christmas morning, "These are the pants that Santa's elves made for you for Christmas." My Ole Miss uniform was now complete. I wore those pants every time I played football with my friends Johnny Woodward, Lance Greer, and Flournoy Anderson.

After a few years had passed by, my family moved to Oak Ridge, Tennessee, in 1953. That move was absolutely devastating for me. Even more devastating, my football pants didn't make the move. They were unintentionally left behind in Louisville, never to be seen again.

Fast forward to the Ole Miss versus Mississippi State football game in Jackson, Mississippi, in 1988, forty-five years after my move to Oak Ridge. Our oldest son, Bryan, was the Ole Miss placekicker, team captain, and leading scorer for the Rebels.

Following the game, Judy and I were on the field celebrating the Ole Miss victory with Bryan. Suddenly, up came two gentlemen carrying a Piggly Wiggly brown paper grocery sack. They were State fans, all decked out in maroon and white.

Lo and behold, it was Johnny Woodward and Flournoy Anderson, two of my best friends as a young boy in Louisville. We hugged and cried at being reunited for the first time since my gut-wrenching move away from Louisville. As Johnny handed me the brown paper sack, he said, "Sam, you left these at my house when you moved. I found them recently when I was cleaning out my attic, so Flournoy and I are so happy to bring you your Ole Miss football pants." Then they both said to me, "We're so proud that you got to wear the real ones like your son is wearing today."

This story just proves that boyhood friendships run deep in Mississippi. I'm prouder of these pants than anyone can comprehend. Why? These pants helped my life-long dream come true. I got to wear the real Ole Miss Rebel football uniform and play for the Red and Blue! This story also energized me to compose this little verse:

I'm a Rebel, Through and Through.
Even My Blood Runs Red and Blue.
There's Nothing Finer in this Land,
Than a Loyal, Obnoxious, Ole Miss Fan!
Samuel Walton Owen
Nickname: Soupbone
Ole Miss Rebel Football Player 1959-1962
#60 in Your Program, #1 in Your Heart
Judy's Husband
Ole Miss Sweethearts Forever!

"The Pants" are now where they should be. They are framed in a large shadow box, hanging on the wall of our home in Oxford, Mississippi, the home of Ole Miss and our beloved Rebels. Hotty Toddy!

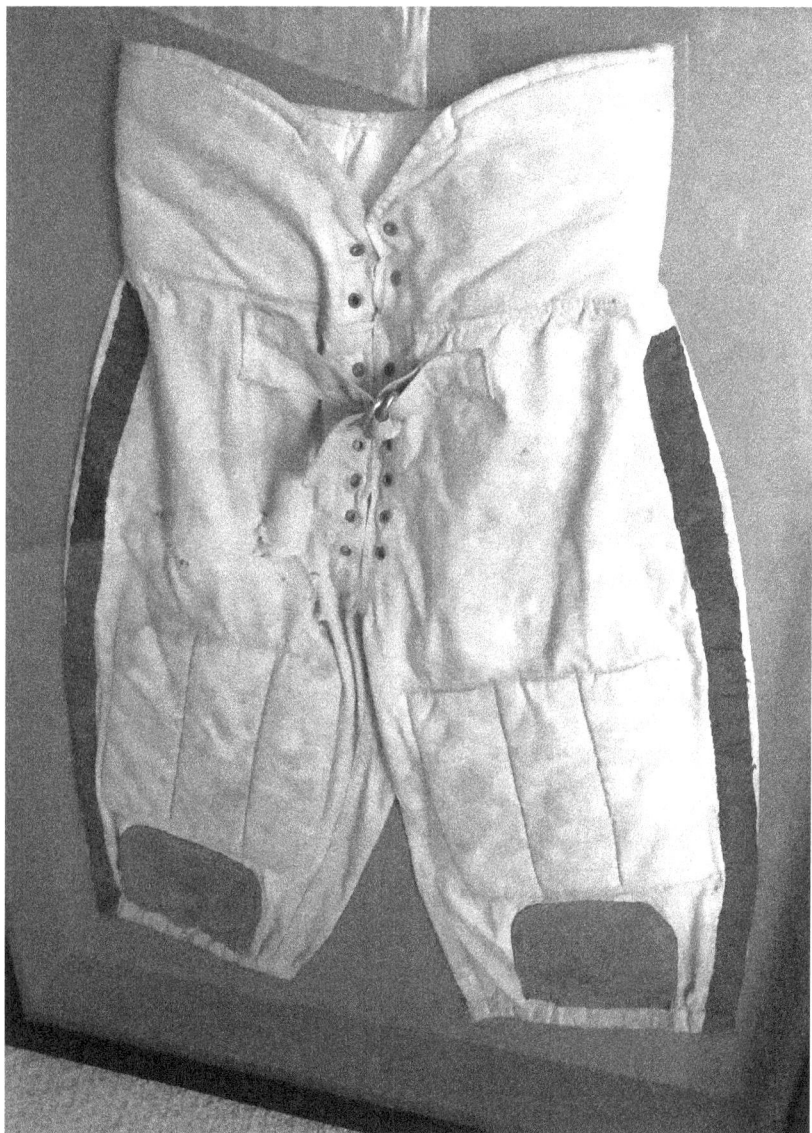

Boyhood Friends Reunited by the Fiddlin' Stick

My late friend Tommy Cato and I were the only two people left on the planet who knew what The Fiddlin' Stick was and how to use it.

The inventor of this magical, ingenious gadget was none other than my daddy, Samuel Walton Owen, Sr. Sadly, he has passed on to the big lake in the sky, but my memories of him haven't. They will last forever in my heart until I join him on high.

The Fiddlin' Stick is one of those things in life that has a special meaning to dear friends and no one else. This is a true story about Tommy and me. It's about our long and enduring friendship. It's a story about two Mississippi boys who had the privilege to grow up during America's rejuvenation after World War II. But the most important part of our life was a fishing pole, not world wars or commerce. Now, let me tell you about The Fiddlin' Stick.

The odds are quite heavy against you knowing what a Fiddlin' Stick is. That's not because you are stupid. It's because I knew only four people in the world who knew what a Fiddlin' Stick was: Daddy, Tommy's Uncle Boyd Pickens, Tommy, and me.

Tommy and I lived in New Albany, Mississippi, at the time. We were both born in Mays Hospital. I was born first because Tommy was thirteen months younger. Our mamas were best friends and played bridge together at least two or three times a week.

Uncle Boyd and Daddy were best friends and serious crappie fishermen. Their favorite fishing hole was the vast waters of Sardis Lake near Oxford.

Daddy and Uncle Boyd often took Tommy and me fishing on Sardis Lake during those hot Mississippi summers. We always took several Fiddlin' Sticks with us each time we went fishing in case we broke or lost one. Plus, we wanted lots of hooks in the water with a lively, shiner minnow on it. Hey, those fabulous fishing poles were our secret weapons.

Here's how we made The Fiddlin' Sticks. We would find or buy a long fishing pole made from a rather long, stiff bamboo pole that had little eye screws embedded in each joint of the cane pole down to a foot above the small reel that contained the fishing line. The line ran through those eyes and was weighted down with a large lead sinker a foot above the hook. That configuration allowed us to pull the hook with the minnow attached to it to the very end of the pole so we could stick our Fiddlin' Stick into the thick, willow treetops of Sardis Lake.

Then we would drag out enormous, slab crappie that loved to dine on the shiner minnows we used for bait. More often than not, those big slabs weighed in excess of two pounds. The Fiddlin' Stick was our top-secret weapon that we kept to ourselves.

Daddy and Uncle Boyd also built a huge minnow vat in Boyd's oversized garage to house the minnows we used for bait. Tommy and I helped seine for those little shiner minnows in the numerous creeks and brooks in our neck of the woods.

Now, you're wondering about the pertinence of this story about a fishing pole. That's to be expected. For this story, it has total relevance and sentimental value to me. It did for Tommy as well. So, here it is.

I joined Hospital Corporation of America (HCA) in 1973 and came to Nashville in 1985 as President of HCA's Physician Services Company. One day, Tommy Frist, Jr. called me and asked me to interview a fellow who was being considered a new employee for HCA's Information Systems Division. Of course, I agreed. The reason I was interviewing this fellow was to confirm that he would fit within the culture of HCA, which was sacrosanct to the company.

On the day of the interview, this big guy walked into my office. After shaking hands, we sat down to talk. Prior to this day, we had met briefly at a high school football game and attended some of the same social functions. Otherwise, we didn't know each other.

We went through the usual chit-chat to break the ice and get acquainted. From time to time, I thought to myself that I may have known this fellow from some other time and some other place, but nothing was certain.

Then I asked, "Tommy, where did you grow up?"

He said, "I'm from Mississippi." That's how Mississippians say it.

I was astonished and said, "Are you serious? So am I." Then I asked him where in Mississippi. He said, "I was born in New Albany but lived in Jackson."

I was dumbfounded and said with excitement, "I was born in New Albany in Mays Hospital!"

That's when it happened. He told me his mama's name was Katherine Grace Pickens Cato, from New Albany. I was astonished and sat there speechless for several seconds, which felt like several minutes.

Finally, I said, "Your mama was my mama's best friend. They were bridge partners."

Then he said, "My Uncle Boyd Pickens was her brother."

Shocked again! I said, "Your Uncle Boyd was my daddy's best friend and fishing partner."

Then Tommy asked what was in Uncle Boyd's garage.

I said, "A huge minnow vat."

Then he asked me, "What did they fish with?"

My response floored him.

I said, "The Fiddlin' Stick."

That's when we simultaneously realized that we were boyhood friends.

We got up from our seats and hugged each other. That's also when we reunited as best and dear friends until Tommy's unexpected death. Thank God for The Fiddlin' Stick for rekindling a boyhood friendship.

The Storytellers

Let me further explain what a haint is for you city slickers and Yankees. A *haint* is a ghost, an unearthly spirit, pure and simple.

Throughout my life I had heard numerous stories and tales about haints. These stories were related to me by some of the favorite people in my life. Unfortunately, I don't remember all of their tales, but I still reminisce about the storytellers most days of my life.

I can visualize them as vividly as if they were sitting in our kitchen, telling me those wonderful stories today. I have cherished these memories throughout my life. I revisit them frequently with joy and melancholy when I want to relive what I call "Old Times Not Forgotten."

The storytellers were Vergie, Elsie, Angie, Elouise, and Mammy. Those wonderful ladies were our help, and they were considered prominent members of my family. For the uninformed or the politically correct crowd, take a deep breath and relax. "The help" wasn't a derogatory reference. It was truly a term of endearment for the domestic workers, as they are called today. Our help always referred to themselves as the help, and they appeared to be proud of their professional roles in our lives.

They had a pecking order among themselves. The most senior member was at the top of the pecking order and was considered the boss lady, or as they said, "The Head Nigger in Charge." Today it's a sin to say such words. Again, relax. The help often called each other "nigger." We never did. In fact, my mama didn't allow the word to be used in our house.

I still remember the help as some of the dearest friends in my life. They had more love in their hearts than any group of people I have ever known. They said the same thing about us white folks because we were all members of the same big, happy, Southern family.

The help were instrumental in molding my beliefs, my character, and my loving heart. They helped discipline me when I needed to "tune down," and they were always there when I needed a "tune up."

They had a knack for scolding me and making me feel good about it. I don't rightly know why, but I suppose it was because of the post-scolding kitchen treat that always mysteriously appeared even when no favor was asked.

I loved hearing Vergie ask me to do her a favor. She'd say, "Masser Sam, would you do me a fava? Taste one uh dem sausage biscuits o'er yonder and see if it be fit to eat," or she'd say, "Dem drumsticks needs some sho nuf tastin' to make sure day be sho nuff good and crispy. Let's see if day's wuf eatin'."

The tasting never stopped after just one drumstick because I would always cast my shadow-of-a-doubt expression Vergie's way, and she would respond with, "What you talkin' about boy?" Then she would always go through her ritual to find just the right drumstick for the second tasting.

Oh yes, the help could sho nuff cook up some of the best food that ever existed, especially the fried chicken because it was always fried in lard to give it that fabulous flavor and incredible crispiness without a hint of overcooking, burned spots, or greasiness. Colonel Sanders' chicken isn't even on the same planet as Vergie's.

Thank God my daddy owned a chicken farm, because we ate fried chicken several times every week. It's still my favorite meal if it's cooked right. I vowed long ago that if I was ever on death row at Mississippi's brutal prison, Parchman Farm, waiting for the electric chair, my last meal request would be fried chicken, as long as Vergie was doing the cooking.

I only wish that my current family could have known the help because they were instrumental and essential members of my family. God knows I miss them, and I think of them almost every day of my life. I can still hear them laughing and cutting up in our house, especially in the kitchen. I have told my wife Judy numerous times that Vergie wouldn't start working until she fixed breakfast for the two of us so we could eat together.

I can see Vergie now in her starched-white uniform, sounding and looking exactly like Prissy. She entertained me. She introduced me to haint stories that were often scary and always a whole lot funny. She educated me about her life. She helped teach me how to live mine. Vergie and the storytellers loved me, and I loved them.

About the Author

Sam Owen humbly states, "A charmed life can't exist unless you are willing to seize the moment or opportunity and do something with it." In New Albany, Mississippi, on August 4, 1941, a renaissance man was born.

Sam is a dreamer. As a child, he dreamed of playing football for his beloved Ole Miss Rebels and winning SEC and National Championships. Both dreams came true. He saw the Atlantic Ocean for the first time and wondered what was beyond the horizon. He found out when stationed with the Army in Germany from 1964 to 1967. One dream never materialized. Sam never became a pirate like the swashbucklers in Errol Flynn movies.

Sam spotted the love of his life for the first time at Ole Miss in 1959. He knew that he was going to marry that adorable girl someday. He finally met Judith Ann Josephson in September 1960, and they're still courting, kissing each other good night, holding hands, and saying "I love you" after sixty blissful years of marriage.

After earning a master's degree in hospital administration from Washington University in St. Louis, Missouri, he worked in the healthcare industry as an administrator of hospitals and as a corporate executive for Hospital Corporation of America. In 1990, Sam and his business partner acquired Cumberland Health Systems, which they sold in 1994.

Sam's first book is the result of encouragement from two of his favorite people—Judy and one of his wonderful granddaughters, Corinne Owen. Sam finally agreed and here it is, *Old Times Not Forgotten.*

Reminiscing about my Mississippi childhood has brought me great joy, and I hope that my stories have entertained you. —Samuel Walton Owen